extreme
STREETFiGHTER
MOTORBiKES
> the ultimate collection

First published in Great Britain by
Arcturus Publishing Limited
First Floor
1-7 Shand Street
London SE1 2ES

for Bookmart Limited
Registered number 2372865
Desford Road
Enderby
Leicester
LE9 5AD

This edition published 2000

Authors: Steve Logan (and credit to Dave Manning, Nik Samson, Marcus Tyson)
Chief photographer: Simon Everett
Design: Guy Hawkins
Editor: Emma Hayley
Editor-in-Chief: Stu Garland
Original concept: Kaspa Hazlewood, Paul Richards
Printed and bound by: Garzanti Verga S.r.l, Italy

Cover Bike: Chom Scott's GSX-R Harris Magnum IV
End Papers: 1. Stephen Mahler's Spondon GSX-R 110 (front)
2. Naith Gill's Kawasaki RX100 (back)

©Arcturus Publishing Limited

ISBN 1-84193-035-0

STREETFIGHTER

extreme
STREETFIGHTER
MOTORBIKES
> the ultimate collection

Frank Allmann, Simon Everett

ARCTURUS

>iNTRODUCTiON

The Streetfighter Phenomenon   6-11

CHAPTER ONE
>THE NAKED 'FiGHTER

Dodge's GSX-R   14-17
Steve Proudlove-Spondon   18-21
2x Buells   22-25
Harris Magnum IV GSX-R   26-29
Crackle Martek   30-33
Harris Revisited   34-37
Jack's Turbo Bandit   38-41
Specials' Harris   42-45

CHAPTER TWO
>THE FAiRED 'FiGHTER

Marlboro Buell   48-51
Plastic canvas   52-55
Endurance GSX   56-59
Working for the enemy   60-63

CHAPTER THREE
>THE COMPETiTiON 'FiGHTER

Veggie Dave's drag bike   66-69
Wayne's wonder   71-73
Turbo Zed   74-77
Paddy's Harley   78-81
Turbo Katana   82-85
World beating RD   86-89

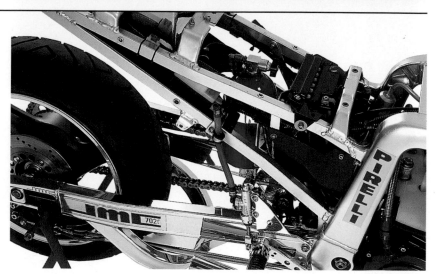

CONTENTS

CHAPTER FOUR
>THE SUPERMOTARD 'FiGHTER

Supermotard threesome   92-95
Revenge DTR   96-99
Super M Yamada   100-103

CHAPTER FiVE
>THE TWO-STROKE 'FiGHTER

Yamaha RD350LC   106-109
Yamaha RD 350   110-113
Gamma RG500   114-117

CHAPTER SiX
>THE ULTiMATE

V-Max in gold   120-123
Sculpture Ducati   124-127
Rotary Norton   128-131
Jet Trike   132-135

The Triton: the café racer meets the streetfighter

THE STREETFIGHTER PHENOMENON

The spirit of the streetfighter has been around for as long as people have been riding motorcycles. Although it's only in recent years that the 'fighter has been perfected as a form of customising expression, bikes coming straight from the factory are always regarded by a minority of the riding population as mere raw material. These bikes are just a starting point from which to create a wholly unique and much more potent machine than anything on offer in any showroom or shop. The irresistible urge to individualise motorcycles is nothing new, and it has manifested itself in three main genres over the second half of the twentieth century – the café racer, the chopper and the streetfighter.

But even before that, back in pre-war Britain, it was commonplace for the motorcycling enthusiast to ride his bike along to an event, take off the lights and number plates, fit some competition numbers and spend the afternoon racing against other like-minded souls. At the end of the day he would make his way home on the self-same machine that, moments beforehand, he'd just been thrashing mercilessly around a track. This didn't just apply to circuit racing either. It was an era before bikes became too specialised in their roles, a time when virtually any bike could be tweaked and tuned to compete in road racing, sprints or even trials. And they were... in their hundreds and thousands.

The Fifties and Sixties saw the birth of the racetrack-influenced café racer, a machine conceived by the youth of the era to enable them to imitate on the street their short circuit racetrack heroes. Since these bikes were used by their owners to travel at speed from one riders' meeting place – usually a café – to another, they were very soon dubbed 'café racers'. The rules were simple: a stock motorcycle would be stripped to the bare bones and fitted with a huge aluminium petrol tank with matching seat, swept-back exhaust pipes with open or reverse-cone 'mega' silencers, alloy wheel rims and mudguards, and clip-on handlebars and rear-set foot controls to give that all-important race-inspired riding position.

Even though almost any make of bike could be given the café racer treatment, the favoured machines were 500 and 650cc twins from Triumph, BSA and Norton, with maximum street credibility being accorded to genuine race-developed road bikes like the BSA Gold Star, Manx Norton and Velocette Thruxton. Top of the road bike tree was the Triumph Bonneville engine and gearbox, slotted into rolling gear from the featherbed-framed 500cc Manx Norton, thus creating the famed 'Triton'. Ironically, the Featherbed frame was based on a design created by Rex McCandless to take a Triumph power unit, and it was only because Norton factory rider Artie Bell knew from personal experience how well the frame handled that Norton employed McCandless to build the frames for them. But as Manx Norton frames were not the cheapest or the easiest chassis to find, the vast majority of roadgoing Tritons were built using the similar Featherbed frame from the 600 and 650cc Norton Dominator range.

THE STREETFIGHTER PHENOMENON

As the Sixties drew to a close and motorways started to blight the land, the truck drivers' cafés and 'greasy-spoon' catering establishments that had been the traditional A-road haunts of the café racers were disappearing fast. This coincided with the arrival on the world scene of fast and reliable machines from the Land of the Rising Sun. Beginning with the four-cylinder Honda CB750, closely followed by the Kawasaki Z900, there followed a flood of high performance machines such as Suzuki's GS750 and 1000, Honda's CBX1000 and Yamaha's XS1100, to name but four. Tuned British engines, though, continued to win accolades in competition circles, most notable of which was Tom Christenson's twin Norton Commando-engined 'Hogslayer' that dominated US drag racing, culminating in a sub-eight-second, 170mph run over the quarter mile.

The four-cylinder Japanese motorcycle gave speed freaks the world over access to the sort of power that had previously been the sole preserve of works factory race teams and the very rich. With the availability of the Honda CB750 and the mighty Kawasaki Z900, anybody, but anybody, could slap a deposit on the counter of their favourite dealer and ride away on a machine that could out-perform just about anything else on the road. And just as aftermarket and performance gurus such as Colin Seeley, Paul Dunstall, Dave Degens (aka Dresda) and the Rickman brothers had produced aftermarket parts for home-brewed specials such as the Triton, so they continued to make frames and go-faster equipment for the less fragile Japanese machinery.

It was on the drag strip that the Japanese in-line fours first made their mark, as the poor handling qualities of those early mega-horsepower bikes just didn't matter when the target was simply to go as fast as possible in a straight line. Proof of the potential lurking within Japanese motors came when, in 1975, the eight-second barrier was broken by Russ Collins on his injected nitro, triple-engined, Honda-powered drag bike 'Atchison, Topeka and Santa Fe' with 7.92 seconds at 178mph over the standing quarter mile. To this day, the record-breaking drag bikes have always been based, however tenuously, on Japanese engines.

Although the new wave of Japanese machinery was quick in a straight line, on the racing circuits it was a different story. Its all-conquering engine power was limited by the lack of development of the rolling chassis – 100bhp is next to useless if frames are going to flex badly under the mildest of cornering stress. In order to tame the wild handling characteristics of the Japanese bikes, specialists such as Dunstall, Dresda and Read Titan started to offer fork braces, cast alloy wheels with higher quality European tyres and shock absorbers and box section swinging-arms. Rickman and Seeley even offered complete frame kits side-by-side with traditional race parts such as big petrol tanks, little seats, loud exhausts and clip-on handlebars.

It was at this time that the term 'Superbike' was first coined. The Superbike racers came from the US, where production racing was held in much higher regard than the World Championship GP series that the Europeans favoured. Even though Steve McLoughlin won the first national meeting, held in Daytona in 1976, on a BMW R90S, it was the big, butch and brutal in-line fours of Yamaha, Suzuki, Honda and Kawasaki that were the real crowd pleasers. They were roadster replicas of production models – two-wheeled bar-room brawlers that spawned all-time classic muscle bikes such as Eddie Lawson's green Kawasaki Z1000, the blue and yellow Moriwaki Zed of Graham Crosby, Wes Cooley's Suzuki GS1000 and Freddie Spencer's Honda CB900.

These bikes were first seen in the United Kingdom during the TransAtlantic Match races of the Seventies, where a team of American racers would visit Britain in a series of six races on three separate circuits over the Easter weekend. The likes of Kenny Roberts and Barry Sheene rode 2-stroke GP bikes, but the midfield was made up of the high-barred 4-strokes, with Cooley's GS1000 amongst them. The style of these racetrack refugees spilled out on to the streets with plenty of home-brewed Superbike clones being rapidly put together by an inspired bike-riding public. Kawasaki got in on the act, too, with their production Z1000 replica of Lawson's mean, green machine.

Strangely enough, while the Japanese factories had begun to produce more and more powerful multi-cylindered engines, the laid-back image of the chopped custom motorcycle and its associated lifestyle was gaining momentum. As the low budget film 'Easy Rider' hit the screen on both sides of the Atlantic, so every biker with an urge to be different turned for inspiration to the chopped Harley-Davidson Panheads of Peter Fonda and Dennis Hopper. It was a cult that was to endure, and in order to capitalise on its widespread appeal, the mighty Japanese motorcycle manufacturers and the revitalised Harley-Davidson Motor Company began to fall over themselves to produce a plethora of `Factory Customs.' These copied and diluted the street presence and aggression of the backyard-built chopper and its siblings such as the lowrider.

Although the custom motorcycle had very little in common with performance motorcycles, it was a descendent of the custom scene that was the first kind of bike to bear the monicker 'streetfighter'. Low-slung and complete with a four or six-cylinder, large capacity engine that was tuned to the hilt, stripped to the minimum and devoid of rear suspension, they drew their styling from all-out drag bikes rather than the Easyrider-style chopper. When the owners spent money on their machines it was on engine improvements and not paint or other cosmetic enhancements. These bikes were built with one purpose and one purpose only. To go very, very quickly in a straight line ... usually to the next pub.

The release of the alloy-framed, oil-cooled Suzuki GSX-R750 in 1985 at last gave the ordinary biker the chance to sample the delights of a bike that was a true racetrack replica. The original GSX-R 750 was based on

THE STREETFIGHTER PHENOMENON

the endurance racing XR69, built specifically by Suzuki and not available to the public. As brake horsepower figures broke through the 100bhp barrier, 'power for the people' became a maxim that was never easier to come by. To make full use of that power, aftermarket frames and running gear were still obligatory.

Aesthetically speaking, the perfect frame for a streetfighter may still be considered to be one of the immaculate examples of steel or alloy trelliswork from Spondon or Harris, but it has to be said that the Japanese have come a long way from the Superbikes of the Seventies with their spongy suspension and flexing frames. So much so that the power and handling prowess of almost any modern sports bike has a limit of performance that is far above and beyond the riding capabilities of the average owner.

The handling of the Kawasaki Zeds and GS/GSX Suzukis, which were favourites in the Eighties and still rule on the drag strip, can indeed be transformed by the addition of upside-down forks, single-sided swinging-arms and the ubiquitous three-spoke cast alloy wheels, with their attendant floating discs and multi-piston brake calipers. However, it's also a fact that, despite their favourable power-to-weight ratios, many home-built modern creations, complete with the most up-to-date rolling gear, may never achieve the supreme poise and handling of factory bikes such as the Honda FireBlade, the Yamaha R1 or Kawasaki's ZX12.

One thing that cannot be denied is that style comes from the street. The home-brewed café racers of the Fifties influenced race-styled production bikes such as the BSA Rocket Gold Star and the Norton 650SS in the Sixties. In a similar way, the Japanese factories jumped on the chopper bandwagon in the late Seventies in an attempt to get a piece of the custom pie, with an array of disappointing and downright ugly factory customs. In the late Eighties, the Big Four Japanese manufacturers had recognised the popularity of retro-styled, naked, large capacity bikes and duly produced bikes to suit, but they were bikes which were but a meek and timid reminder of the sort of machines the public yearned for. In recent years, Kawasaki, Suzuki, Yamaha and Honda, Italian bike producers Ducati and Cagiva, and even the formerly staid Hinckley Triumph have taken a long, hard, sideways glance at the contemporary craze for the stripped-down streetfighter. Each has created a watered-down imitation that, in the tradition of the factory custom, lacks the street style and originality of the raw aggressive bespoke backyard originals.

What is the future of the streetfighter? Well, the original streetfighter ethic of making a standard engine more powerful, bracing the frame and swingarm, and fitting wider, stickier tyres on wider, lighter and more rigid three-spoke wheels is becoming redundant. The only way to improve the new breed of factory bikes with attitude is to fit components that are of a quality equal to that fitted to World Championship Superbike or

Grand Prix machines. As we get further into the new millennium, those factory 'fighters are coming more to resemble the street bikes they were intended to emulate. Kawasaki's Eddie Lawson replica features the engine from the 190mph ZX12 to replace the underpowered ZRX1100; Honda have the (overweight) X11; Cagiva have the Suzuki TL1000-powered Raptor and V-Raptor; Ducati are making a Monster with the water-cooled 916 engine to replace the old air-cooled SS lump, and so on.

As engines are now as powerful as any road riders can cope with (although the idiom 'too much is never enough' will always apply), and chassis are capable of containing the requisite amount of horsepower, it only leaves the styling to be improved upon. Whether there will be a return to the stripped-down race replica – witness the over-abundance of GSX-R1100s in the early Nineties – or whether more elaborate styling will come into vogue – as practised widely in France – it seems likely that the days of the frame kit are numbered. The demand for specialist frames to improve handling has evaporated as the manufacturers have fine tuned both design and production processes, to the point where the chassis of even a basic factory 'fighter is capable of keeping the wheels of, say, a big bore, nitrous-fed machine in line.

It would be fair to say that things have come full circle from the days of the café racers of the Fifties to the streetfighters that are now ridden by a new generation of highway hooligans. The parallels between the two are obvious. Both were built from the fastest bikes of their respective age and both species were modified to be faster, lighter, meaner, cleaner and more outrageous-looking than anything a manufacturer of out-of-the-crate motorcycles had to offer. But most of all, unlike the chopper and its customised clones, both the café racer and the streetfighter were, and are, singularly European in concept and owe nothing at all to the Transatlantic 'form-before-function' ideology of the contemporary Seventies' chopper and its offspring.

There have, though, been converts to the streetfighting cause around the world. The Americans currently favour huge power outputs, billet wheels and extended swinging-arms, particularly in the Southern States, due to the popularity of drag racing. The Germans have a preference for gaudily-painted engines and very short, stubby, kicked-up tail units. The French are partial to over-the-top paintwork and body styling, while the British like their high-barred, naked, bug-eyed, attitude-laden power-houses.

Fashion and technological advances will determine how and when those trends progress, and which direction they will ultimately take, but one thing is certain. While motorcycles exist (legislation permitting), there will always be those imaginative obsessives out there intent on making them more outrageous, more anti-social, more extreme. Welcome to the world of the Streetfighter.

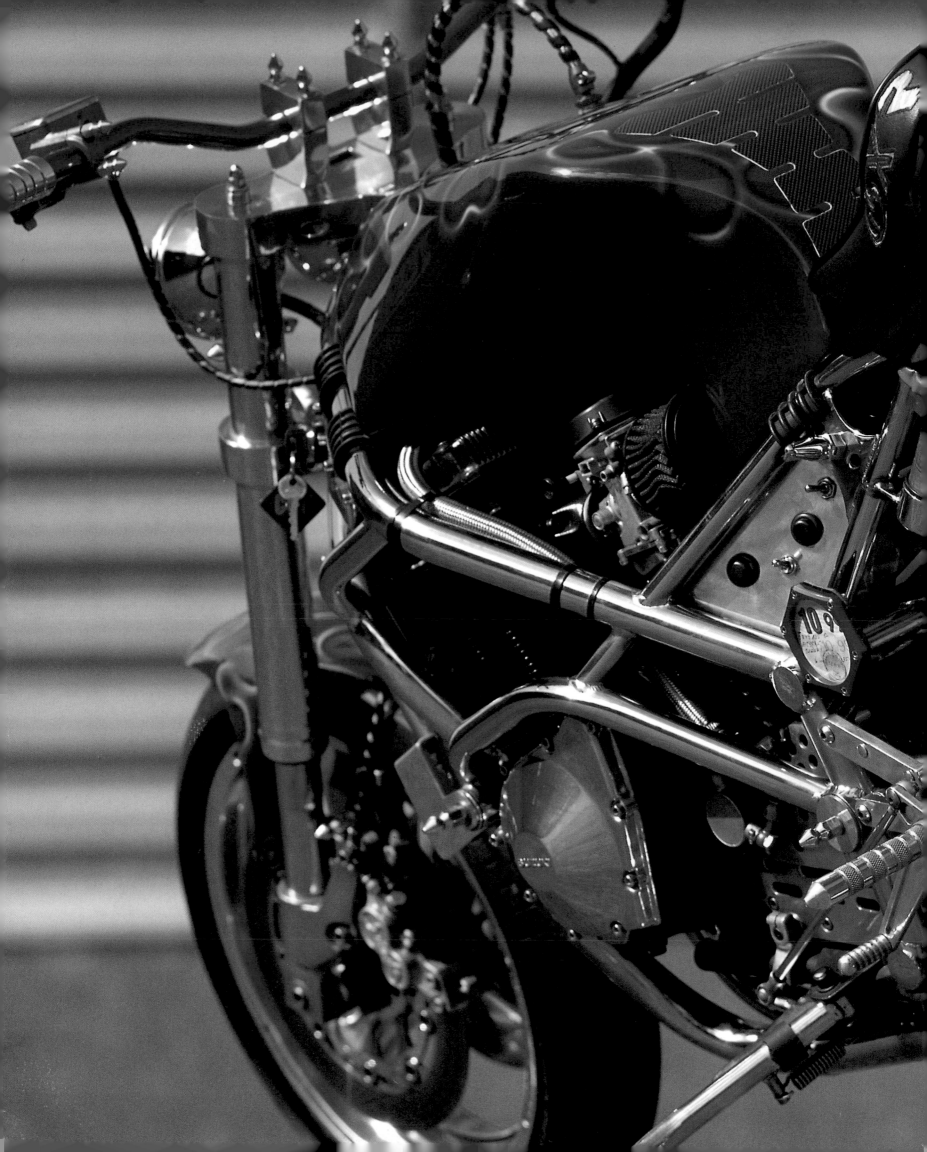

THE NAKED 'FiGHTEr

Dodge's GSX-R

ENGINE: COSWORTH 1340CC, 9:1 COMPRESSION RATIO, PORTED AND POLISHED CYLINDER HEAD, APE SLOTTED SPROCKETS, HEAVY-DUTY CYLINDER HEADS STUDS/NUTS, HEAVY-DUTY CRANKCASE BOLTS, LOCK-UP CLUTCH, ONE-OFF OUTRIGGER PLATE, KOSMAN OFFSET GEARBOX SPROCKET, DYNOJETTED SUZUKI GSX-R 1100M CARBS, K&N FILTERS, VANCE & HINES PRO-PIPE.

FRAME: 1996 SUZUKI GSX-R 1100H WITH ONE-OFF DRS SUBFRAME, BRACED HEADSTOCK, INSIDE TOP FRAME RAILS PLATED IN FOR STRENGTH, OFFSET SWINGARM PIVOT ON L/HAND SIDE, MARTEK REARSETS

FRONT END: SUZUKI GSX-R 750M FORKS (REWORKED BY MAXTON), DRS YOKES, KERSHAW 120X17" SPLIT RIM WHEEL, RENTHAL BARS, SUZUKI GSX-R 750WP CLOCKS

REAR END: SUZUKI GSX-R 750WT SWINGARM & SHOCK, HONDA FIREBLADE FRONT CALIPER, SUZUKI GSX-R 1100M DISC, KERSHAW 7X17" SPLIT RIM, 200 SECTION TYRE

BODYWORK: CARBON FIBRE SUZUKI GSX-R 750M FRONT MUDGUARD, SUZUKI GSX-R 1100H TANK WITH MODIFIED BASE AND RELOCATED PINGEL FUEL TAP, HONDA CG125 TAILPIECE.

ELECTRICS: SUZUKI GSX-R 750WP SWITCHGEAR AND LOOM, KAWASAKI GPZ1100 B2 HEADLIGHT, YAMAHA RD500LC REAR LIGHT, HONDA FIREBLADE BATTERY

DODGE'S GSX-R

IT'S POSSIBLE TO KEEP IT UP IN TOP GEAR ON ONE WHEEL – ALL THE WAY TO 130MPH AND BEYOND...

Similar to many bikes built before by Dodge, its owner, this Suzuki was built to pull wheelies. Big, long, high, fast and impressive wheelies. Originally run with a 1186 (2 mm oversize on 1127 barrels) motor, it's now fitted with a Cosworth 1340 kit which had lain unused for some time by a friend of Dodge's until a deal was struck and cash changed hands. Dodge fitted it together with slotted cam sprockets, heavy duty cylinder studs, nuts and crankcase bolts, a lock-up clutch, new (stock) conrods and big-end shells and a Vance & Hines Sidewinder Pro-Pipe. The cylinder head had already been gas-flowed, but underwent a further stage of polishing and porting to suit the larger pistons.

Dodge decided that the usual black paint job on the engine just wasn't good enough any more, so he painstakingly blanked and masked every single bit of the motor and had it powder coated gloss black. It resulted in a fantastic finish, but beware – this kind of thing takes about eighty hours to achieve because, if just a single grain of blasting sand gets inside, it's goodbye to the engine. The chances are that it will seize in the first few minutes of newly-rebuilt running.

With the engine finished, it was time to get to work on the chassis. The first port of call was to one Tony Kershaw, well-known drag racer and top engineer, to acquire a new rim for the Kershaw rear wheel. Dodge had already bought a 200 section rear tyre and needed a huge 7-inch rim to put it on... However, the GSX-R 1100H frame isn't wide enough to accommodate a 7-inch rim, so an entirely new, one-off back end was fabricated which, by using a 750 SRAD swingarm and shock and offsetting the lower left side of the frame, enabled the rim and tyre to fit nicely. With an out-rigger bearing and a Kosman offset sprocket, the chain now just about clears the left-hand edge of the tyre, but only just.

With all of it finished and back on the road, and after some judicious preparation on the rolling road, the GSX-R produced 105ft/lbs at 6000rpm and 155bhp at 8000rpm – at the back wheel. With this kind of output, Dodge is able to hold it just on the back wheel through the gears all the way to fifth, and it's possible to keep it up there, too, on one wheel – all the way to 130mph and beyond...

Steve's Spondon

ENGINE:	SUZUKI GSX-R 1100M, STAGE 3 DYNOJET, MODIFIED MICRON STAINLESS STEEL 4-2-1 SYSTEM WITH NO END CAN, DYNA COILS, TAYLOR LEADS, GOODRIDGE WIDE COOLER AND LINES, MODIFIED SUMP TO HOLD EXHAUST
FRAME:	SPONDON BIG TUBE ALLOY FRAME WITH DETACHABLE SUB FRAME
FRONT END:	WHITE POWER UPSIDE-DOWN FORKS, SPONDON ADJUSTABLE YOKES, SPONDON 320MM DISCS, VTR1000 FRONT WHEEL, DUCATI 916 CALIPERS, SPEEDO FROM ANDY B'S CELLAR, BRIDGESTONE BT50 TYRE, ZXR MASTER CYLINDER, GOODRIDGE BRAKE LINES
BACK END:	SPONDON GULL-ARM SWINGARM WITH 6 INCH REAR WHEEL ADJUSTERS, ÖHLINS SHOCK, VTR1000 WHEEL, DUCATI MONSTER REAR CALIPER WITH MODIFIED HANGER, GOODRIDGE BRAKE LINE, BRIDGESTONE BT50 TYRE
BODYWORK:	SPONDON ALUMINIUM TANK, MODIFIED DUCATI 916 FRONT MUD GUARD, MODIFIED DUCATI MONSTER SEAT AND COWL

STEVE'S SPONDON

Back in the late Seventies, various frame manufacturers applied their talents to the test of competing against, and beating, the factory teams on race circuits around the globe, building chassis capable of out-handling the factory offerings – the TZs, TRs and KRs – giving both factory and privateer riders the choice of expensive, but flexible, factory originals or cheap and taut home-grown replacements. Some of these builders moved on to more profitable ventures like kit cars (Rickman) or to specialise in certain areas like suspension (Maxton), but others continued to fabricate frames, some for the track (Harris), and some for the road like this GSX-R-engined Spondon – Steve Proudlove's shiny, understated, minimal yet radical GSX-R-engined Spondon.

It's a machine that is very deceiving as, although the bike looks as though it's very rarely used and kept as a poser's show-only bike, the fact is that it has been used in anger across the length and breadth of Europe – as well as up the drag strip – with complete reliability (except for the occasion when it dropped its oil cooler in France).

With an attitude similar to road-going supermotards – those motocrossers with 17-inch wheels and sticky tyres – the Spondon shouts 'fun'. The low weight from the aluminium frame, swingarm, subframe and fuel tank, and minimal painted carbon-fibre bodywork, married to the torque-laden 1100cc GSX-R engine, mean this bike will perform huge crossed-up wheelies and will slide the rear tyre from side to side when making a departure.

But it's that colour-changing blue-green paint that really finishes this Spondon off and makes it stand out from all the others currently to be seen across the country. It's a colour normally seen only on certain very exclusive British sports cars.

Although it has a relatively standard 1100M motor – just the usual minor additions like K&N filters, a Dynojet kit, Dyna coils, Taylor leads and a free-flowing exhaust – this Spondon is capable of having a serious go at any opponent, and Steve fancies doing a bit more straight line action on the drag strip with the Spondon in the future, hence the six-inch rear wheel adjustment built into the swingarm. And he's got a big bore kit ordered and on its way, too.

WITH AN ATTITUDE SIMILAR TO ROAD-GOING SUPERMOTARDS –THOSE MOTOCROSSERS WITH 17-INCH WHEELS AND STICKY TYRES –THE SPONDON SHOUTS 'FUN'.

Monty Python

ENGINE	1998 S3 THUNDERBOLT (1200 SPORTSTER), BUELL RACE KIT - THUNDERSTORM HEADS, BUELL RACE EXHAUST
FRAME	1998 BUELL S3 THUNDERBOLT
FRONT END	1998 BUELL S3 THUNDERBOLT, UPSIDE-DOWN FORKS, 17-INCH WHEEL, 6-POT BUELL CALIPER BY PERFORMANCE MACHINE, SINGLE FLOATING DISC
REAR END	1998 BUELL S3 THUNDERBOLT, WHITE POWER SHOCK.

Tigerstripe

ENGINE	1998 BUELL S1 LIGHTNING (1200 SPORTSTER), STAGE 1 HIGH-FLOW AIR FILTER, VANCE & HINES EXHAUST
FRAME	1998 BUELL S1 LIGHTNING
FRONT END	1998 BUELL S1 LIGHTNING, UPSIDE-DOWN FORKS, 17-INCH WHEEL, 6-POT BUELL CALIPER BY PERFORMANCE MACHINE, SINGLE FLOATING DISC
REAR END	1998 BUELL S1 LIGHTNING, WHITE POWER SHOCK.
BODYWORK	1998 BUELL S1 LIGHTNING WITH MODIFIED REAR 'GUARD

A BRACE OF BUELLS

THOSE WHO'VE RIDDEN ONE WILL HAVE HAD THEIR PRECONCEPTIONS ABOUT HARLEY MOTORS BEING SLUGGISH CHALLENGED QUITE FIRMLY.

The Buell might be regarded by some as evidence of the Harley-Davidson Motor Company's recognition that the motorcycling world was moving on while they'd been slumbering for longer than was commercially prudent, and their 'fightered Sportster shows just how much notice big business takes of trends on the street. Make no mistake, the Buell is positive proof that Harley have, for reasons best known to themselves and the worthy souls who set the standards for US exhaust emission laws, been hiding away a little gem in the Evolution Sportster engine, long derided as the 'entry-level' Harley in the States and the 'second-best' to the Big Twin in Europe. All of a sudden H-D, by default maybe, had on their hands an admittedly odd-looking bike, but one that in a single fell swoop ought to have silenced the detractors (and a huge, huge thank-you to Erik Buell here for his faith in a product which, for some time, had a less-than-enthusiastic reception from the bods on the board).

Those who've ridden one will have had their preconceptions about Harley motors being sluggish challenged quite firmly. The beachhead was established in 1996 with the S1 Lightning – truly, you'd get 135mph before the rev-limiter cut in, and riders would perform inadvertent, and unavoidable, wheelies away from even the most innocuous of traffic-light hold-ups. All this with only a few minor cylinder head modifications to the valve seats and a (fairly benign) carb that had simply been tuned in properly. There was no magic, but it did make you wonder why they hadn't seen fit to try the formula before they did.

Here we have two examples of the marque which rely for their impact not so much on the sporty pretensions associated with the word 'Streetfighter', but on their livery. It's relatively early days yet for somebody to have produced an out-and-out, front-to-back, top-to-bottom, 100% customised Buell, so we'll have, for now, to be satisfied with what will turn out, I'm sure, to be a pair of trailblazers in their field. These two come courtesy of owners John Potter and Dockgate 20 H-D/Buell, along with painter Steve Woodhall.

John's Thunderbolt, resplendent in its 'Monty Python's Flying Circus' paint job, has been treated to a Buell race kit, which comprises a pair of potent Thunderstorm cylinder heads, a stainless racing exhaust system, a free-flow air filter and suitably jetted carb, while Dockgate 20's Lightning – though equally vibrant in the paintwork department – benefits from the Stage I tuning package of a less restrictive air filter, carb jetting and a Vance & Hines 2-into-1 exhaust. There will be more engine modifications to come, too, you can be sure of that, just as there will be more and more 'fightered Buells on the streets as the months go by.

THERE WILL BE MORE ENGINE MODIFICATIONS TO COME, TOO, YOU CAN BE SURE OF THAT, JUST AS THERE WILL BE MORE AND MORE 'FIGHTERED BUELLS ON THE STREETS AS THE MONTHS GO BY.

Harris Magnum iV GSX-R

ENGINE:	SUZUKI GSX-R 1100L, STAGE THREE DYNOJET, K&N FILTERS, ONE-OFF STAINLESS EXHAUST, DYNA COILS,136BHP
FRAME:	HARRIS MAGNUM IV, MODIFIED SUBFRAME
FRONT END:	SUZUKI GSX-R 1100L FORKS, WHEEL AND BRAKES, A&D ENGINEERING YOKES AND RISERS, BUILT-IN MINI SPEEDO, RENTHAL 'BARS, A&D ENGINEERING GRIPS
REAR END:	HARRIS SWINGARM, ÖHLINS SHOCK, SUZUKI GSX-R 1100L WHEEL AND BRAKE, HARRIS MASTER CYLINDER
BODYWORK:	SUZUKI GSX-R 1100L FRONT MUDGUARD, HARRIS MAGNUM IV FUEL TANK, MODIFIED KAWASAKI Z650 TAILPIECE, SUZUKI BANDIT TAIL-LIGHT

HARRiS MAGNUM iV GSX-R

WHAT DiFFERENTiATES CHOM'S MAGNUM iV FROM EVERY OTHER RUN-OF-THE-MiLL HARRiS — iF THERE COULD EVER BE SUCH A THiNG — iS THE STYLiNG.

It's now just about thirty years since Steve and Lester Harris, along with their good friend Steve Bayford, set up the now world-renowned Harris Performance Products Ltd. In that time, barely more than three thousand bikes have rolled out of the Hertfordshire-based Harris HQ. Those bikes include machines that have competed in GPs, World Superbikes, World Endurance, and the Isle of Man TT. And, of course, there are numerous privateer bikes that have competed in domestic championships, not to mention the legions of road bikes based around Harris frames...

But, in spite of the countless accolades accorded to the competitive side of Harris Performance Products, they are probably better known for the range of road bike frame kits, from the Magnum I through to the Magnum VI, encompassing engines from the humble Kawasaki GPz550, to the Honda FireBlade and the king-of-the-hill Suzuki GSX-R 1100, as seen here. Even these types of road-going bikes, though, have been developed using the expertise gathered from the company's racing exploits.

Chom Scott is the owner of one such road-going Harris, but his example appears a touch different from the usual. The frame is the normal Magnum IV – a

steel peripheral lattice arrangement – surrounding an oil-cooled GSX-R engine, and held off the ground by an all-Suzuki front end and huge Harris swingarm, Öhlins shock and Suzuki wheel and brake at the rear. The engine itself doesn't hold many surprises either – a torquey and powerful, but very standard, version of the 1100 GSX-R, with only the addition of some free flowing filters, a Dynojet kit, Dyna coils and a one-off exhaust with high-level exhaust can to give the right sound and feel.

What differentiates Chom's Magnum IV from every other run-of-the-mill Harris – if there could ever be such a thing – is the styling. There's the modified Z650 tailpiece that looks so small behind the expanse of aluminium Harris fuel tank, lending the bike a look reminiscent of the German style of 'tail-high' street-fighter. The high and wide Renthal handlebars provide a riding position akin to that of a motocrosser, as do the thick billet aluminium yokes and risers that hold them. The bike is finished in a way that would make many custom bike owners green with envy. The way that every bare aluminium part, and every bit of stainless steel is polished to a lustrous sheen; the way pike nuts are used throughout the bike; the way the leather seat has the GSX-R logo stitched into it and the sublime and subtle paintwork all make it a dream.

Crackle Martek

ENGINE: SUZUKI GSX-R 1100N, STAGE THREE DYNOJET, K&N FILTERS, MICRON 4-2-1 WITH SHORTENED COBRA END CAN, SERCK MARSTON OIL COOLER AND LINES

FRAME: MARTEK MK 2 BIG TUBE, MARTEK FOOTRESTS AND HANGERS

FRONT END: SUZUKI GSX-R 1100N ALBRAFIN-COATED FORKS, POLISHED YOKES, WHEEL, BRAKES, MASTER-CYLINDER, SWITCHGEAR AND CLOCKS, ÷HLINS STEERING DAMPER, RENNTEC DRAG 'BARS, CARBON/ALLOY CLOCK SURROUND

REAR END: MARTEK BIG TUBE OVER-BRACED SWINGARM, TECH 2000 SHOCK, SUZUKI GSX-R WHEEL AND BRAKE, HARRIS MASTER-CYLINDER

BODYWORK: SUZUKI GSX-R 1100N FRONT MUDGUARD, MARTEK FUEL TANK WITH AEROTEK FLUSH FILLER, ONE-OFF FIBREGLASS SEAT UNIT BY EVESHAM STREETFIGHTERS, BRANCATTO CLOSED CELL RACE FOAM SEAT

CRACKLE MARTEK

IN THE RICH AND VARIED WORLD OF MOTORCYCLES, AND EVEN WITHIN THE NARROWER FIELD OF STREETFIGHTERS, THERE EXISTS NATIONAL VARIETY WITHIN THE STYLES.

In the rich and varied world of motorcycles, and even within the narrower field of streetfighters, there exists national variety within the styles. For example, the Americans like low and long, stretched bikes, the French like wild, gaudy paint schemes on faired bikes, and the Germans like short stubby tail units, just like Russell Garrett's Martek you see here. Russell Garrett isn't German, however, and you can tell the Martek isn't German because the engine hasn't been painted in a bold primary colour.

The bike's skeleton comes in the form of a Martek MkII 'Big Tube' frame. Martek are now defunct, but while they were in business, they were a firm which specialised in producing aluminium frames and CNC-machined components. The same company also supplied an over-braced swingarm, an aluminium fuel tank, and footrests and hangers. Once he'd found a complete GSX-R 1100N, which furnished him with the rolling gear and engine, Russell had constructed a rolling chassis and an engine that was yet to be fitted along with all the ancillaries. So, at the wheel

of his boss's van, he made the trip to Evesham Streetfighters Engineering so that they could get on with the task of assembling the various boxes of bits into a complete motorcycle, thus freeing Russell from the swearing and scuffed knuckles involved in a bike build. A few months later Russell paid another visit to Evesham in order to collect his now running Martek GSX-R.

As well as placing the engine within the chassis, the Evesham SF crew had also fabricated the clock pod, risers, chainguard, undertray, and seat unit; modified the subframe, exhaust can and rear wheel, as well as connecting up all the electrics, bodywork, brakes, oil cooler, etc, to the point where the bike was a runner. All that was now needed to complete the project was the paint and the polish. The finishing touches were applied by Florida Racing who polished the forks and yokes, while Derek of Didcot buffed the wheels and applied the House of Kolor-sourced paint, a base of silver metalflake covered with the Vreeble that gives the bike that stunning crackled finish.

Harris Revisited

ENGINE: SUZUKI GSX-R 750M, ALBRAFIN ENGINE COVERS, K&N STAGE 3 FILTERS, MICRON STAINLESS STEEL EXHAUST, CARBON FIBRE CAN, GOODRIDGE OIL COOLER, GOODRIDGE LINES WITH ANODISED FITTINGS, STAINLESS AIR FILTER SURROUNDS, ENGINE & EXHAUST MOUNTING BRACKETS BY OWNER

FRAME: HARRIS MAGNUM I, MODIFIED BY OWNER TO ACCEPT GSX-R MOTOR AND GSX-R RISING RATE REAR END, WELDING BY SWEARY BOB AT SPONDON, HARRIS MAGNUM IV STYLE REARSETS, ALUMINIUM SUB-FRAME AND STEERING DAMPER BRACKETS BY OWNER

FRONT END: SUZUKI GSX-R 750WP FORKS, YOKES, WHEEL AND BRAKES, GSX-R CLOCKS WITH HARRIS CARBON FIBRE POD, ALUMINIUM RISERS WITH RENTHAL BARS, MAXTON 916 STEERING DAMPER

REAR END: COMPLETE SUZUKI GSX-R 750WP REAR END, REAR SHOCK RE-WORKED BY MAXTON, HARRIS MINI REAR MASTER CYLINDER, BLUE ANODISED REAR SPROCKETS, REGINA GOLD CHAIN

BODYWORK: HARRIS CARBON FIBRE MUDGUARD, HARRIS MAGNUM IV STYLE TANK WITH FLUSH FILLER, HARRIS ROTAX SEAT UNIT WIDENED BY 40MM. DECALS, SEAT PADS AND EMBOSSING BY OWNER

HARRIS REVISITED

QUITE SIMPLY, THE 'H' MEN ARE AMONGST THE VERY BEST CHASSIS BUILDERS IN THE WORLD.

The name 'Harris' was always going to figure quite prominently in any book about the streetfighter genre of motorcycle, so it should come as no surprise to see this particular machine included in the line-up, another example that makes extensive use of the 'H' word in its technical specification. The company has been producing replacement frames for the discerning speed freak for years now, and today, cult members can be found in all corners of the globe, from Stockport to Sydney, from Rotherham to Rio. So there must be a reason for such dedication … and there is. Quite simply, the 'H' men are amongst the very best chassis builders in the world, and they have been since they began. Even though they've been perfecting their craft for several decades on an ongoing basis, such is the integrity of the product that even an early model like this one of Pete Dawson's can still compete almost two decades later.

Originally built for racer Jim Wells' Kawasaki Z1000, the Harris Magnum I now accommodates a Suzuki GSX-R 750M engine, and does it quite comfortably too, handling the extra power of the modern motor as though it had been specifically designed for it. The running gear has been uprated, however, which can't be a bad thing. A complete GSX-R front end, for instance, was added to the formula to improve the steering and suspension at the sharp end, though the back end proved to be a little more difficult to deal with. The frame had been built to take a cantilever swingarm/shock set-up, but Pete's plans included a rising rate 750WP arrangement, so he employed the talents of Sweary Bob at Spondon to carry out the necessary modifications to their usual high standards.

With the basic skeleton done, dusted and promising to deliver sublime handling, it was time to start looking at the aesthetics and the detail which can make or break a project (and which is all-too-often overlooked in the rush to get a bike out of the workshop and on to the tarmac). Pete declined to go a more obvious route with the bodywork, choosing instead to take a Harris Rotax seat unit and widen it by 40mm to suit the rest of the bike just so, while his attention to detail is exemplified by the Ducati 916 Maxton steering damper brackets and the neatly-made stainless steel air filter surrounds. The paintwork, too, shows careful thought – gaudy, bold livery was never an option here, despite the amount of time and effort that had gone into building this bike. Rather, Pete chose an understated and beautifully finished black and blue pearl scheme that no photograph can really do justice to. A fitting flourish to a finely-built, exceptional streetfighter.

Jack's Turbo Bandit

MAKE & MODEL:	SUZUKI BANDIT 1200
ENGINE:	SUZUKI GSX-R 1100, 1277CC, MTC PISTONS, COMPRESSION RATIO 8.2:1, SQUISH CLEARANCE OF 0.040'', CARILLO RODS, KENT CAMS, SLOTTED CAM SPROCKETS, GAS-FLOWED HEAD, UNDERCUT GEARS, LOCK-UP CLUTCH, RAYJAY F40 TURBO, ATP RACE INLET MANIFOLD, S&S CARB, MR. TURBO WASTEGATE, 'WUNOFF' EXHAUST, WATER INJECTION
FRAME:	SUZUKI 1200 BANDIT
FRONT END:	SUZUKI BANDIT 1200 FORKS AND WHEEL, WHITE POWER SPRINGS, PFM 320MM DISCS, PFM SIX POT CALIPERS, GOODRIDGE HOSES
REAR END:	SUZUKI BANDIT 1200 WHEEL, BRAKE AND SWING-ARM, WHITE POWER REAR SHOCK
BODYWORK:	SUZUKI BANDIT 1200
ELECTRICS:	SUZUKI BANDIT 1200, TURBO LOOM
PAINTWORK:	MILLENNIUM BIKE PAINT
POLISHING:	HOLESHOT RACING
THANKS TO:	'JOHN AT WUNOFF EXHAUSTS, PAUL MEREER AT PFM, TONY FROM MILLENNIUM AND 'TOO TALL' PAUL FOR PRINTING ALL OF HOLESHOT'S LITERATURE...'

JACK'S TURBO BANDIT

IS TWO HUNDRED AND FORTY-EIGHT BRAKE HORSEPOWER WITH A MASSIVE 158LB/FT TORQUE ENOUGH?...

For nigh on fifteen years, Jarrod 'Jack' Frost has been involved in the two-wheeled high performance world, from road racing and drag racing to becoming a big fish in the stunt riding pool, as well as achieving the World Wheelie Speed Record on the Isle of Man ... and now to tuning.

Suzuki's 1200 Bandit is the most popular bike to be used among the streetfighter hordes — the engine's already good-looking and powerful, the basic aesthetics are just right, there are hundreds of them around in various states of repair, and most of all, they're cheap.

But having one that stands out from the masses requires either a ridiculously gregarious paint-job or an immensely powerful engine. Being the proprietor of Holeshot Racing, it's no surprise that Jarrod avoided the multi-hued, costly paintwork and went down the horsepower route.

Is two hundred and forty-eight brake horsepower with a massive 158lb/ft torque enough? If not, then you can have two hundred and eighty-one brake horsepower with an unbelievable 168lb/ft torque instead. Just wind open the Mr Turbo's wastegate from 15psi (248bhp) to 20psi, and that'll give you a comprehensive 281bhp.

And it's not just a case of bolting the turbo onto the standard twelve hundred Suzuki motor, either. Turbo engines need to run a lower compression than normally aspirated engines to prevent the huge heat increases present from pre-igniting the combustible inlet charge (supplied from the S&S Shorty carb) and melting the pistons. So MTC Turbo pistons have been used to lower the Bandit's compression right down to 8.2:1 (standard is around 11:1), the gas flow is improved by a flowed head and ATP inlet manifold, while the bottom end is held together with the aid of Carillo con rods, a lock-up clutch and undercut gears.

With all that extra power, the Bandit's handling needed looking at, so the front forks were treated to White Power fork springs and a matching White Power shock was fitted at the rear. And whenever those 281 equines threaten to get out of hand there's a set of PFM brakes to call upon. 320mm narrow pad track discs with a pair of six pot calipers ensure that this most brutal of Bandits stops (almost) as well as it goes.

SUZUKI'S 1200 BANDIT IS THE MOST POPULAR BIKE TO BE USED AMONG THE STREETFIGHTER HORDES —THE ENGINE'S ALREADY GOOD-LOOKING AND POWERFUL, THE BASIC AESTHETICS ARE JUST RIGHT.

Specials' Harris

ENGINE:	HONDA CBR900RR, STAGE 3 DYNOJET KIT, K&N FILTER IN STOCK FIREBLADE AIRBOX, AKRAPOVIC DOWNPIPES, SPECIALS MID-SECTION & CAN
FRAME:	HARRIS MAGNUM II, SPECIALS FOOTRESTS, HANGERS & ENGINE MOUNTS
FRONT END:	HONDA CBR900RR FORKS, WHEEL, BRAKES, MASTER-CYLINDER, SWITCHGEAR, CLOCKS & SURROUND, HARRIS YOKES, SPONDON HANDLEBARS
REAR END:	SPONDON TUBULAR GULLARM, ÖHLINS SHOCK, SUZUKI GSX-R 750 WHEEL, SPONDON DISC, BREMBO CALIPER
BODYWORK:	CARBON FIBRE HONDA CBR900RR FRONT MUDGUARD, APRILIA RS250 FAIRING, SPONDON RC45-STYLE PETROL TANK, MODIFIED HONDA CBR900RR RACE SEAT UNIT

SPECIALS' HARRIS

YOU DO HAVE TO REMEMBER THAT IT'S HOUSED IN A FRAME THAT'S LIGHTER THAN AIR, AND THE POWER-TO-WEIGHT RATIO IS MUCH MORE IMPORTANT THAN OUTRIGHT POWER ANYWAY.

There are certain people, and certain shops, who continue to create stunning streetfighters year in, year out. Each spring a new creation rides forth from their workshops, and this Harris is one such bike. Built by Geraint Short at Specials Glasgow, it's a Harris Magnum II, with a Honda CBR900RR engine. Those people who know their streetfighting onions will know that this should not be possible, as the Magnum II was created by the Harris brothers in the early Eighties, whereas the FireBlade didn't rear its tank-slapping head until 1992. Harris didn't actually jig up a frame for the FireBlade motor until they created the Magnum V in 1997-98.

So, in building this Magnum 'Blade, Specials have had to machine up new engine mounts to hold the Honda lump in the slightly modified Harris frame, and new bracketry was required to hold the standard Honda airbox in its required place, as well as new and up-to-date footpeg hangers and pegs too. Due to the positioning of the airbox, the original Magnum II petrol tank would never have fitted, so an aluminium tank, built by Spondon to an RC45 style, was slapped on. The motor itself is pretty much standard – with Akrapovic exhaust downpipes and a Specials mid-section and Scorpion end can, and a Stage Three Dynojet and K&N filter on the induction side, that's about all the engine mods there are. Although it makes

some 125bhp on the dyno – which isn't a great deal in these days of 150bhp R1s and Hayabusas – you do have to remember that it's housed in a frame that's lighter than air, and the power-to-weight ratio is much more important than outright power anyway.

The front end is Honda FireBlade through and through, with the exception of a set of Harris yokes, between which nestles a pair of Spondon clip-on bars. The rear end is courtesy of Spondon – being a tubular aluminium 'gullarm', looking much more at home than the spindly steel affair that originally graced the Magnum II. Keeping the back end off the ground is a Suzuki GSX-R 750 wheel, with a Spondon disc and a Brembo twin-pot caliper, all supported by a multi-adjustable Öhlins shocker.

The neat half-fairing is from an Aprilia RS250, complete with the two-stroker's headlamp, the front mudguard is a carbon CBR9 item to match the rest of the front end and, keeping it in the Honda family, a FireBlade race seat unit sits on the Harris subframe having been suitably adapted to fit around the high-level exhaust can.

The only thing that wasn't done by Geraint and the Specials team is the black and crimson paintwork, laid on by Duncan Magregor. All of the other work required in the building of this bike – the wiring, the polishing, the spannering, the swearing, the tea-drinking – was 100% Specials.

Marlboro Buell

ENGINE:	1998 BUELL M2 CYCLONE, BUELL S1 MILDLY PORTED HEADS, SCREAMIN' EAGLE CAMS, STAGE 2 DYNOJET KIT, AIRBOX REMOVED, K&N 7" FILTER, STRAIGHT CUT GEARS, SUPERTRAPP SILENCER
FRAME:	1998 BUELL M2 CYCLONE
FRONT END:	STOCK 1998 BUELL M2 CYCLONE FORKS, YOKES, WHEEL AND BRAKES, CLIP-ON 'BARS, QA THROTTLE, MODIFIED CLOCKS
REAR END:	STOCK 1998 BUELL M2 CYCLONE 'ARM, WHEEL AND BRAKE, WP FULLY-ADJUSTABLE SHOCK
BODYWORK:	STOCK 1998 BUELL M2 CYCLONE FRONT 'GUARD, HEAVILY-MODIFIED AIRTECH S1 FAIRING, STOCK FUEL TANK, HEAVILY MODIFIED BUELL S1 SEAT, AIRTECH SINGLE SEAT UNIT AND UNDERTRAY

MARLBORO BUELL

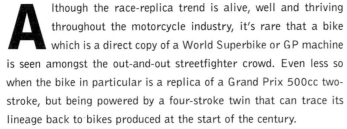

Although the race-replica trend is alive, well and thriving throughout the motorcycle industry, it's rare that a bike which is a direct copy of a World Superbike or GP machine is seen amongst the out-and-out streetfighter crowd. Even less so when the bike in particular is a replica of a Grand Prix 500cc two-stroke, but being powered by a four-stroke twin that can trace its lineage back to bikes produced at the start of the century.

Although fairly radical looking, it's a glowing testament to the quality of the standard Buell that the majority of this stunning bike is exactly as Erik Buell intended. The visually arresting part of this M2 Cyclone is the race-rep paintwork on the smooth and swoopy bodywork – it's a Marlboro design, which was handled by Dream Machine, and was applied to bodywork that was supplied by a company that produces some of the most dramatic drag, circuit and custom fibreglass components available – Airtech.

As the standard Buell engine is much improved compared with the 1200cc Harley-Davidson Sportster engine upon which it is based, there was very little that was required to be done to the Marlboro Buell as far as performance modifications were concerned, except, of course, for the ubiquitous air filter and exhaust changes that are invariably done to every Buell before it has worn out its first pair of tyres. However, it was decided that replacing the Cyclone cylinder heads with the slightly more radical versions from the later S1 would be a modification worth doing, particularly if the S1 heads were gas-flowed before they were fitted. Some 'fast road' Screamin' Eagle cams have also replaced the standard Buell ones, while the breathing has been sorted with a SuperTrapp exhaust, as well as the airbox being removed and the standard carb being fitted with a Stage 2 Dynojet kit.

All the work on the bike was undertaken by Duncan Peace, who also replaced the original helical gears for straight cut items. Why? Well, just in case the next owner does decide to give the bike some real power in the form of turbocharger, supercharger or (more likely) nitrous oxide, then the gearbox won't end up in pieces scattered down the tarmac.

In order to ensure the Buell stays upright, Duncan hasn't neglected the bike's handling either and, because the front ends on Buells are fairly good as standard, the mods extend merely to replacing the rear shock with a fully adjustable WP item. And just in case you think that this bike won't be used on the road because it has got no lights, then look again. Hidden behind the fairing is a 5.5" Cyclops headlight, tucked behind the screen to prevent the lines of the fairing being spoiled.

ALTHOUGH FAIRLY RADICAL LOOKING, IT'S A GLOWING TESTAMENT TO THE QUALITY OF THE STANDARD BUELL THAT THE MAJORITY OF THIS STUNNING BIKE IS EXACTLY AS ERIK BUELL INTENDED.

Plastic Canvas

ENGINE:	GASFLOWED HEAD, STAGE 3 DYNOJET KIT AND K&N FILTERS, HEAVY DUTY CLUTCH SPRINGS, STAINLESS COBRA RACE PIPE
FRAME:	MIRROR POLISHED
FRONT END:	MIRROR POLISHED FORKS AND YOKES, WHEEL PAINT BY PIERS DOWELL, GOODRIDGE HOSES
REAR END:	ARM OVER-BRACED BY EVESHAM STREETFIGHTERS (THEIR FIRST), THEN MIRROR POLISHED, WHEEL PAINTED BY MR DOWELL, GOODRIDGE HOSE
BODYWORK:	STANDARD

PLASTIC CANVAS

WHEN THE TIME FINALLY CAME, PIERS WAS TOLD TO PAINT WHAT HE THOUGHT WOULD SUIT, SO THE REST WAS DOWN TO HIS WEIRD AND TWISTED IMAGINATION.

Whenever an owner takes on the idea of modifying his bike, it often happens that they'll have to decide just where to direct the cash, whether it be towards engine work, chassis mods, or cosmetic enhancement. As the GSX-R that David Radcliffe had been running in a rather rough and ready condition was looking somewhat the worse for wear, he decided that his limited funds should go towards improving the aesthetics of the bike.

Having sought financial assistance from his wife, David turned to one of the UK's premier bike painters, Piers Dowell. Piers is well known for his lurid and detailed paint schemes present on many of the Old Country's top show and race-winning streetfighters, so David was disappointed when the realisation struck that he would have to wait six months until Piers had an opening to paint the Suzuki. When the time finally came, Piers was told to do what he thought would suit, so the rest was down to his weird and twisted imagination. And as you can see, Piers didn't disappoint.

Mrs Ratcliffe was kind enough to fund her husband's paint job, and she in turn had her eye on a BMW – a four-wheeled BMW – which thereby limited the amount of money Mr Ratcliffe got each week to spend on the Eleven. Consequently, David had to ensure that any subsequent modifications provided maximum value for money. Fortunately, as he'd got himself the 1100 version of the GSX-R, 140 bhp wasn't far away, in either time or monetary terms.

As anyone who's had experience of extracting more power from the larger capacity GSX-Rs will affirm, the cheapest and most cost-effective way of achieving it is to invest in a jet kit, some free breathing filters and a less restrictive exhaust. And indeed, that is exactly what David bought for his Suzi. And apart from some Goodridge braided steel hoses and a lot of DIY mirror polishing, the only other major enhancement David's limited resources could finance was an Evesham Streetfighter Engineering over-braced swingarm – the first one they ever made.

Fortunately, after a little luck and some hard work, David has at last secured extra funds to indulge some of his more exotic desires for the bike. Whether it be a Spondon rolling chassis, turbo kit or a full-on race-tuned motor, you can be sure it'll make the 'fighter faster, lighter or better looking ... or all three.

Endurance GSX

ENGINE: SUZUKI GSX 750 ET ENGINE, RE-JETTED CARBS, EXHAUST MADE FROM IKEA TABLE LEGS WITH A TL1000 BOSDEMPER CARBON SILENCER, HEAVY DUTY CLUTCH SPRINGS, MILDLY FLOWED HEAD.

FRAME: STANDARD GSX750 FRAME MODIFIED TO TAKE A MONOSHOCK AND FULLY BRACED FOR MORE STIFFNESS. ALL WORK BY OWNER AND GJK TECHNIEK.

FRONT END: MODIFIED ZXR400 UPSIDE-DOWNERS WITH HOME-MADE BILLET YOKES, FIREBLADE WHEEL AND DISC WITH YZF750 6 POT CALIPER ON HOME-MADE SPACER, AP ADJUSTABLE MASTER CYLINDER, ZX7-RR FRONT MUDGUARD AND ALUMINIUM CLIP-ONS.

REAR END: SWINGARM FROM HARRIS F1 WITH 16" DYMAG WHEEL WITH BREMBO CAST IRON DISC WITH AP CALIPER AND NISSIN MASTER CYLINDER, FZR1000 SHOCK MODIFIED BY TECHNO FLEX, ZXR750R LINKAGES WITH RIDE HEIGHT ADJUSTER BY OWNER.

BODYWORK: ULTRA LIGHTWEIGHT RACE FAIRING FROM CBR600 WITH AN XL500R HEADLAMP, POLYESTER FUEL TANK FROM SUZUKI ENDURANCE RACER FITTED WITH AN AIRCRAFT FILLER AND KEIHIN FUEL TAP, TANK MOUNTED ON QUICK RELEASE SYSTEM. YAMAHA TZR125 FACTORY RACE SEAT

ENGINEERING: KEVLAR ENGINE CRASH PROTECTOR, ALUMINIUM SUBFRAME, CHAINGUARD WITH INTEGRATED CARBON MUDGUARD, MODIFIED CBR600 REARSETS, CARBON FIBRE DASH PANEL WITH PUSHBIKE SPEEDO, ALL WORK DONE BY OWNER

ENDURANCE GSX

DRAG RACING IS FAIRLY POPULAR IN EUROPE, WITH THE BRITS PREFERRING BIG JAPANESE FOURS, THE GERMANS VEE-TWINS OF MILWAUKEE ORIGINATION, AND THE DUTCH, WELL, THE DUTCH RACE ANYTHING WITH WHEELS AND AN ENGINE...

Although still not nearly as much as in the States, drag racing is fairly popular in Europe, with the British preferring big Japanese fours, the Germans vee-twins of Milwaukee origination, and the Dutch, well, the Dutch race anything with wheels and an engine... The tracks in Holland are basically dyke roads – very narrow roads that run alongside canals – so they only race one bike at a time, and they're usually only 1/8th mile tracks, so most Dutch drag racers will jump at the opportunity to race up the quarter in pairs. Joost Hillen, owner of this endurance-styled Suzi, is one of the racers who's prepared to travel to the UK to get his head-to-head racing kicks.

With a wheelbase of 1480mm, a weight of 179kg (most of which is the engine and a weight distribution of 47.5% front to 52.5% rear, it's compatible with modern sports bolides – even the super-light R1 weighs 177kilos, fully dry. And that's the factory definition of fully dry – meaning there are absolutely no fluids on board, not even fork oil, so the Hillen bike will, in reality, weigh less than a fully-fuelled R1. The weight reductions have come about with the swift application of angle grinder to frame, and the fitment of many up-to-date, lightweight parts.

The frame itself has been fully braced up and converted to single shock configuration using an FZR1000 shock, ZXR750R linkages and a home-made ride-height adjuster, and incorporates a Harris F1 swingarm to hold the 16" Dymag wheel, cast iron Brembo disc and AP caliper. The front end is a FireBlade 16" wheel with a ZXR7-RR mudguard held in ZXR400 forks, themselves held in home-made billet aluminium yokes. Braking is taken care of by 'Blade discs and Yam YZF750 six

pots. The bodywork is made of lightweight materials, from the race weight fibreglass Yamaha race seat and CBR race fairing, to the ex-Suzuki endurance racer fuel tank, made in polyester and complete with aircraft filler and hi-flow Keihin tap. More weight has been shed by using an aluminium sub-frame, aluminium clip-on bars, kevlar engine covers, one-piece chainguard/mudguard, carbon dash and a pushbike speedo.

Shoving this little lot down the strip is a fairly standard, and admittedly rather tired GSX750 engine. Breathing has been eased with a mildly flowed head, re-jetted carbs, and a Bos carbon can from a TL1000. An old IKEA table was cut about to provide the tubing required for the exhaust. However, Joost has now managed to obtain an ex-Pro Stock GSX1100 engine to fit in the white and blue Suzi. Bored out to 1327cc and giving a full and healthy 175bhp at the back wheel before the nitrous, the bike is sure to better the mid-twelves it was running with the 750 engine.

Working For The Enemy

ENGINE:	1992 KAWASAKI ZXR750R (K1), RACE TECHNIQUES HEAD, KAWASAKI RACE KIT CAMS, CARBS (39MM FLATSLIDES) AND TRUMPETS, HEAVY DUTY CLUTCH PLATES, STAINLESS STEEL RACE DESIGN EXHAUST WITH CARBON CANS
FRAME:	1992 KAWASAKI ZXR750R (K1), DBR FOOTRESTS AND HANGERS
FRONT END:	MARCHESINI WSB MAGNESIUM WHEEL, AP RACING DISCS, AP RACING SIX POT CALIPERS, SHOWA SUPERBIKE FORKS, MODIFIED DUCATI 916 YOKES, BREMBO MASTER-CYLINDER, STOCK KAWASAKI ZXR750R (K1) HANDLEBARS, ELLIOT TACHO IN ALLY PLATE WITH STARTER BUTTON AND IGNITION SWITCH
REAR END:	EXTENSIVELY MODIFIED HONDA NC30 SWINGARM, ONE-OFF PEST/POLYGON ENGINEERING HUB, ÖHLINS SHOCK, MARCHESINI WSB MAGNESIUM 6" WHEEL, BREMBO THUMB-OPERATED BRAKE, ONE-OFF ALLOY SPROCKET AND CARRIER BY PEST/POLYGON ENGINEERING
BODYWORK:	DUCATI 916 FRONT MUDGUARD, DUCATI 916/KAWASAKI ZXR750 MATCHED-UP FAIRING, ONE-OFF ALLOY RACE DESIGN PETROL TANK, ONE-OFF ALLOY RACE DESIGNS SIDEPANELS, DUCATI 916 TAIL UNIT

WORKING FOR THE ENEMY

A MACHINE THAT CONFUSES BYSTANDERS INTO THINKING IT'S A DUCATI ... AT LEAST UNTIL IT'S STARTED, WHEN THE INLINE FOUR CYLINDER HOWL GIVES THE GAME AWAY.

Many riders like to own perfect road-going replicas of works WSB bikes, whether they be YZF Yams, 996 Ducatis, Suzuki GSX-Rs or Kawasakis like Akira Yanagawa's, which is how this bike started life. An ex-race ZXR 750RR in standard green, white and blue colours, it sported a D&D exhaust and a combination of road and race kit parts. Its owner, Roy, evidently didn't like the look of the works Kawasaki, so he developed his idea of the perfect ZXR.

Roy stripped the bike to its bare essentials. The single-sided arm, a Honda NC30 item, was fitted after being extensively braced and modified. The hub was machined from billet aluminium to accept a Ducati 916 wheel, and the whole bike reassembled with a Ducati 916 seat unit and painted in yellow and white like the Ducati 748.

After about six months, a pair of WSB Marchesini magnesium wheels came Roy's way, along with a pair of fully floating AP Racing discs. It was time to go back to the operating table. The whole bike was torn down once more for the various modifications to be made to the swinging arm – the Marchesini wheel was wider than the 916 wheel, and it also required modifications to the hub, as the drive peg and wheel centre were slightly different from the standard 916 parts. This proved to be a convenient time to do some alterations to the engine,

which included fitting the race kit cams, carbs and inlet trumpets, as well as gas-flowing the head and throwing in some heavy duty clutch plates.

The bike was then reassembled with a new alloy sub-frame by Race Design, a rear shock with adjustable ride height and adjustable tie bars, an adjustable swing arm pivot, a thumb-operated rear brake and a one-off stainless steel exhaust system with a carbon can. The wiring loom has been completely stripped, with the kill switch moved onto the fairing, and only the one switch on the left handlebar for the lights. The dashboard consists of an Elliot Electronic tacho, a starter button and a Z650 ignition switch. Nothing else. The throttle assembly is from a Yamaha YZF750 and Showa Superbike forks were used on the front end. In the interests of weight reduction all the bolts and fasteners on the bike are titanium, and to reduce weight still further, they have been line bored in non-stress areas. Many of the brackets, including the sidestand, are also titanium.

At this time a 916 headlamp fairing assembly was purchased and fitted to the modified ZXR750 side fairings. This, along with the aluminium sidepanels and the rest of the bodywork, was then painted in the works Duke-lookalike candy apple red over a gold base with white pearl inlays, resulting in a machine that confuses bystanders into thinking it's a Ducati... at least until it's started, when the inline four-cylinder howl gives the game away.

Veggie Dave's drag bike

ORIGINAL MACHINE:	SUZUKI GSX1100F
ENGINE:	SUZUKI GSX1100F, 1216CC, GSX-R CAMS, FLOWED HEAD, HEAVY-DUTY CLUTCH, HEAVY-DUTY CYLINDER STUDS, 38MM MIKUNI CARBS, STAGE THREE DYNOJET, NOS NITROUS SYSTEM, V&H COMPETITION EXHAUST, DYNA 2000 IGNITION SYSTEM AND COILS
FRAME:	STEELHEART ENGINEERING 'SPACE AGE', TWO PETROL TANKS (ONE IN TOP TUBES, THE SECOND IN SUBFRAME)
FRONT END:	SUZUKI GSX600F FORKS, 3-SPOKE WHEEL, FULLY FLOATING DISCS, FOUR-POT CALIPERS, STEELHEART YOKES
REAR END:	KAWASAKI ZXR750 5.5" WHEEL AND CALIPER, STEELHEART SWINGARM WITH BUILT-IN AIR SHIFTER RESERVOIR
BODYWORK:	KATANA ONE-PIECE TANK AND SEAT UNIT FROM CHRIS RICHARDS' MOTORCYCLES, SEAT PAD BY OWNER

VEGGIE DAVE'S DRAG BIKE

This bike was conceived as a custom bike, but one that would perform as well as it looked, to streak away from the lights at the drag strip as well as it attracts approving looks on the street, to be reliable yet visually stunning, to achieve ten-second quarter mile times while still being ridden to and from race meetings. It was built by Dave Green as a project bike for the custom bike magazine 'Back Street Heroes', and it has succeeded in all of those aims.

The frame is a one-off steel trellis wrapped around a Suzuki GSX1100F (the

Powerscreen model), complete with steel swingarm that holds the 5.5" ZXR rear wheel and contains the air shifter reservoir. Although the shocks have been replaced by struts to form a rigid rear end, the swingarm runs on rose-jointed bearings to enable the bike to be raised or lowered to tune the chassis for the track, while the front end is Suzuki GSX600 throughout. As the bodywork is a one-piece glass-fibre affair, there is no conventional fuel tank. There's a small tank incorporated within the frame tubes that holds six pints (three quarts), but that's more than adequate

FOR ROAD USE THERE'S A REMOVABLE TWO AND A HALF GALLON TANK THAT SITS BELOW THE SEAT.

for quarter-miling. For road use there's a removable two and a half gallon tank that sits below the seat.

The GSX engine was bored to 1216cc using Wiseco pistons, and treated to a pair of GSX-R cams, a flowed head, a heavy duty clutch and cylinder studs, a Dyna ignition and a NOS nitrous oxide kit, with breathing taken care of by 38mm Mikuni carbs, with a Dynojet kit, and a Vance & Hines exhaust. The completed bike was then sent off to the painters and stove-enamellers to have the frame, swingarm and wheels enamelled in candy blue, and to have the bodywork painted in the striped and marbled blue by Geoff Ridgeway. Then it was just a matter of fine tuning.

All didn't go according to plan though, as rather than storm into the Tens (or even the Elevens) first time out at England's York Raceway, the Suzuki-mounted Dave could only manage a lowly 13.49 seconds at 77mph... Fortunately, this was improved upon a couple of months later when, with a set of borrowed flat-slide carbs, he ran a 10.99 at 128mph. Into the Tens at last, but only just.

Wayne's Wonder

MAKE & MODEL:	1991 SUZUKI GSX-R1100
ENGINE:	ROGER UPPERTON GAS FLOWED HEAD, STAINLESS OVERSIZE VALVES, PRECISION MACHINE VALVE SPRINGS, 1216CC WITH JE PISTONS, 13.5:1 COMPRESSION RATIO, HEAVY DUTY CAMCHAIN, RS38 FLAT SLIDE CARBS, CARILLO RODS, MRE LOCK-UP CLUTCH, VANCE & HINES PROPIPE, NOS NITROUS KIT, ORIENT EXPRESS CYLINDER STUDS AND NUTS, DYNA 2000 IGNITION, HEL EXTRA-WIDE 19-ROW OIL COOLER AND LINES.
FRAME:	STOCK, POLISHED AND CHROMED STOCK FOOTRESTS AND HANGERS, SPRINT STEERING DAMPER
FRONT END:	STOCK FORKS SHORTENED 30MM INTERNALLY BY MAXTON, M1R FORK SPRINGS, STOCK WHEEL, POLISHED RIM, SPONDON FLOATING DISC, MINI SIX-POT CALIPER.
REAR END:	JMC 9" OVER DEEP-BRACED SWINGARM WITH 4" SLOTTED ADJUSTERS, STOCK SHOCK MODIFIED BY MAXTON AND 75% STIFFER, STOCK WHEEL, ONE-OFF TORQUE ARM WITH INTEGRAL BRAKE LINE.
BODYWORK:	STOCK FRONT 'GUARD, TWIN OUTLET PINGEL HI-FLOW TAP FITTED TO TANK, ENLARGED TANK BREATHER, FIBREGLASS ONE-PIECE SEAT UNIT AND RACE FAIRING.
ELECTRICS:	DYNA 2000 IGNITION, SHIFT LIGHT, AND COILS, FZR400 RIGHT-HAND SWITCH GEAR, INDUCTIVE SCITSU TACHO, MRE AIR SHIFTER, TWIN BATTERIES.
PAINT:	BY MARK REYNOLDS AT TRIC TRAX, BASED ON THE STANDARD SUZUKI 1100N DESIGN.
POLISHING/PLATING:	WHEEL SPINDLES, ENGINE MOUNTS, BOLTS, FOOTRESTS, ALL SUSPENSION BOLTS AND BRACKETS BY NYPHOS IN CREWE, ALL POLISHING BY OWNER AND PAUL A
ENGINEERING:	EXTRA BATTERY BOX, ELECTRICS TRAY, FAIRING BRACKET, NITROUS BOTTLE BRACKET, CHAINGUARD - ALL FABRICATED. WHEEL SPACERS BY OWNER, ALL OTHER BITS BY OWNER, PAUL, DAVE WALLIS, PETE WILLIAMS AND JEFF HILL

WAYNE'S NOT-SO-LITTLE WONDER

Wayne Little's love of drag racing started in 1989 when he was a race mechanic. Although he'd always aspired to race, he tragically suffered a horrific bike accident on the road and many thought he'd never walk again. Through his own determination he started walking, and then riding again. In 1997, his aspirations were achieved when he began racing – and promptly won the Streetfighters Straightliners 10.90 championship in his first year. This was on a basic stock bike. With an unexpectedly successful debut into drag racing (recording a best of 10.72secs at 133mph), it seemed only natural to continue, but with an improved bike.

So the winter of 1997/1998 was dedicated to rebuilding the bike, making it lower, longer, and more powerful by some judicious engine work and the addition of a nitrous oxide kit into the bargain. Tuner Roger Upperton took time out from preparing ProStock bikes to gas-flow the head and fit stainless steel oversize valves, complete with Precision Machine heavy-duty valve springs. Bored out to suit the 81mm JE pistons, the compression ratio's been measured at a hefty 13.5:1.

The rest of the motor is similarly well thought-out – a heavy duty cam chain, Mikuni RS38 flatslide carbs with 50mm bellmouths and a Yoshimura heatshield, Carillo con rods, MRE lock-up clutch, Vance and Hines ProPipe, undercut gearbox dogs and the aforementioned NOS nitrous kit. The expense didn't extend through the whole engine though, as the cams and crank remained standard items, proving adequate for his existing needs, although the cams may need to be changed for lumpier items if Wayne wants to get into the eight second bracket.

The alternator has been removed, which means that two batteries are required – one for the ignition and the other to power the nitrous system. Held together with Orient Express heavy duty cylinder studs and nuts, kept cool and reliable with a HEL extra-wide 19-row oil cooler and matching lines and breather, and having the fires lit by a Dyna 2000 ignition and coils with Taylor leads, the big Suzuki kicks out a more-than-impressive 165bhp. And that's without the nitrous! That gives an additional 60bhp...

With the engine slung back into the chassis, complete with the nine-inch longer than stock JMC swingarm, shortened forks, re-sprayed and logoed bodywork, re-manufactured brackets and spacers and all the other sundry bits and pieces, the bike took to the track for the 1999 season, with Wayne running a personal best of 9.60secs over the quarter mile, topping out at 160mph and winning the Straightliners Championship class as well.

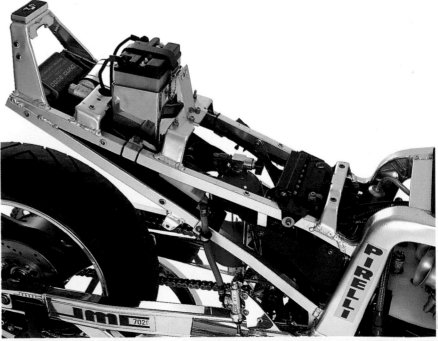

THE BIKE TOOK TO THE TRACK FOR THE 1999 SEASON, WITH WAYNE RUNNING A PERSONAL BEST OF 9.60SECS OVER THE QUARTER MILE, TOPPING OUT AT 160MPH AND WINNING THE STRAIGHTLINERS CHAMPIONSHIP CLASS AS WELL.

TURBO ZED

Turbo Zed

ENGINE: KAWASAKI Z900A4, CAMMOTION TURBO/NITROUS CAMS, OVERSIZE VALVES, ORIENT EXPRESS H/D VALVE SPRINGS, APE BRONZE VALVE GUIDES, WISECO GORILLA 1400CC BLOCK, WELDED, PINNED AND BALANCED CRANKSHAFT, MRE LOCK-UP CLUTCH ASSEMBLY, MODIFIED KOSMAN OUTRIGGER BEARING SUPPORT, RAJAY TURBOCHARGER, MR. TURBO PIPEWORK, S&S CARB, DYNA 4000 IGNITION

FRAME: SPONDON BIG TUBE ZED DRAG CHASSIS, REWORKED HEADSTOCK ANGLE, ADJUSTABLE RIDE HEIGHT, SPONDON FOOTREST HANGERS, SPONDON REARSETS, CANTILEVER MONOSHOCK, ONE-OFF SIDESTAND BY TODDY

FRONT END: KAWASAKI Z900 CLOCKS, GENUINE Z900 GRIPS & SWITCHGEAR, SPONDON ADJUSTABLE YOKES, BILLET RISERS WITH BUILT-IN TURBO BOOST GAUGE, SPONDON HEADLAMP BRACKETS, KAWASAKI ZXR 750 FORKS, WHEELS AND MASTER-CYLINDER, HARRISON SIX POT CALIPERS, GOODRIDGE LINES

REAR END: SPONDON DOUBLE TUBE DRAGRACE SWINGARM WITH SIX-INCH DRAG SLOT EXTENSIONS, ÖHLINS SHOCK ABSORBER WITH REMOTE RESERVOIR, KAWASAKI ZX-7R WHEEL, 200 SECTION PIRELLI TYRE, BREMBO MASTER-CYLINDER, KAWASAKI ZXR CALIPER, GOODRIDGE LINES

BODYWORK: KAWASAKI ZXR 750 FRONT 'GUARD, KAWASAKI Z900 FUEL TANK WITH AIRCRAFT FILLER, Z900 SIDEPANELS SPLIT-PINNED ON, MODIFIED Z900 TAILPIECE WITH HIDDEN TAIL-LIGHT, EDDIE LAWSON SEAT UNIT MODDED TO FIT OVER BOOST AND NITROUS CONTROLLERS

YES, THAT'S RiGHT, THiS iSN'T JUST A SHOW BiKE – iT'S OUT THERE RACiNG ON THE STRiPS AND HiTTiNG THE ROADS iN ANGER TOO.

If there's one thing that can be said about the builders of genuine Streetfighters, it's that they don't do things by halves. Sean Mills, builder of this Spondon Turbo Zed, and proprietor of Big CC Racing, is one of those men. Just check out the spec of this engine, and you'll see what we mean.

At the bike's heart is a piano-wired Wiseco Gorilla block displacing 1400cc with turbo pistons and Teflon buttons, atop which is a Kawasaki Z900A4 head, ported and flowed and converted to eight spark plugs (two per cylinder), with Cammotion turbo/nitrous cams, REC 1.5mm oversize stainless inlet valves, REC 1mm oversize stainless exhaust valves, an APE shim-under-bucket conversion with APE titanium retainers, Orient Express h/d valve springs, Orient Express slotted cam sprockets degreed-in for turbo application, APE bronze valve guides, and reworked combustion chambers.

The bottom end comprises Z900A4 crankcases, milled out to accept the liners, and a welded, pinned and balanced crankshaft with a lapped-on rotor assembly, all held together with heavy duty APE cylinder studs and crankcase studs. Connecting bottom to top in a kinetic fashion is a Tsubaki camchain with an APE billet manual camchain tensioner. A heavy duty clutch and plates, with an MRE lock-up clutch assembly, supply the motive force to the undercut gearbox complete with Orient Express billet second gear, APE kickstart cover, and modified Kosman outrigger bearing support assembly with offset 630 sprocket and Izumi dragrace chain.

The motor's lifeblood is supplied by a Rajay turbocharger with strengthened spring plate for nitrous application, flowed intake manifold, Mr Turbo pipework, S&S Shorty carb, Goodridge turbo oil lines, billet bellmouth and carb adapter plate with nitrous injectors, Hahn Racecraft progressive boost control box and solenoids, Goodridge oil cooler and lines, Goodridge fuel lines, TMC Highpower fuel pump and Pingel dual outlet fuel tap. Sparks come courtesy of a Dyna 4000 drag race ignition with two-stage retard mechanism operated by a Dyna boost pressure switch and the nitrous trigger, and activated by a Dyna Pro-Series ignition timing crank trigger. There's also a Big CC Racing water/methanol system to combat pre-ignition, and in case the 1400 turbo isn't quite powerful enough, there's nitrous oxide supplied by TMC Highpower solenoids, themselves controlled by a Schnitz progressive nitrous controller. This also allows a TMC Highpower nitrous shifter with inbuilt nitrous tank to look after the gear-changes. There may be some Kawasaki parts still left in there somewhere, but not very many.

As for the chassis, Sean sourced most of the running gear from Spondon Engineering in Derbyshire, who are responsible for the Zed's big tube chassis, its adjustable yokes, the drag-spec swingarm (complete with built-in crankcase breather and water-injection tanks) and numerous other small but essential items. The frame itself, which at the time was only the second Zed frame Spondon had done, has been altered from standard dimensions – raked at the front for more stability, and fitted with a one-off cantilever monoshock suspension system. This is designed to allow the chassis to transmit more of the engine's power through the 200 section rear tyre and down onto the road when Sean takes the Zed drag racing. This isn't just a show bike – it's out there racing on the strips and riding the roads in anger too.

Paddy's Harley Hillclimber

ENGINE: 1232CC, SHORT-STROKE, 4-VALVE FEULING HEADS, MODIFIED S&S CRANK IN DELKRON CASES, S&S SUPREME DUTY RODS, 90MM COSWORTH FORMULA ONE RACE CAR PISTONS, SHORTENED & BORED BARRELS WITH BERYLLIUM RINGS (NO HEAD GASKET), 2 X WEBER IDF 40MM TWIN-THROAT CARBS, ONE-OFF INTAKE MANIFOLDS, TITANIUM EXHAUSTS, INTERSPAN RACING IGNITION (NO EXTERNAL POWER SOURCE REQUIRED)

TRANSMISSION: QUAIFE FOUR-SPEED WIDE RATIO GEARBOX, BOB NEWBY BELT PRIMARY WITH ALLY CLUTCH AND FRONT PULLEY

FRAME: ONE-OFF BY OWNER/WELBRO ENGINEERING, 7020 ALUMINIUM TWIN BEAM STYLE SWINGARM HEAVILY MODIFIED SUZUKI 1100 SUSPENSION

FRONT: KAYABA GRAND PRIX UPSIDE-DOWNERS

REAR: KAYABA GRAND PRIX, TITANIUM SPRING WHEELS 17-INCH MARCHESINI MAGNESIUM GRAND PRIX BRAKES AP RACING GRAND PRIX CALIPERS, CARBON FIBRE OR STEEL DISCS

TYRES: MICHELIN GRAND PRIX, WETS, INTERMEDIATES OR SLICKS. 130 X 17 FRONT, 180 X 17 REAR

PADDY'S HARLEY HILLCLIMBER

'LET'S FACE IT, A ONE-GALLON FUEL TANK AND FIVE MILES PER GALLON ISN'T THE PRODUCT OF A RATIONAL MIND...'

This Harley hillclimber was built by one of the few people experienced, capable and committed enough in the UK – anywhere, in fact – to produce such a unique and efficient machine. Paddy Hook's the man responsible, and his credentials in the field of extracting every last ounce of power from the internal combustion engine are impeccable, having in his CV stints of employment in development work with Formula One racing car teams.

As far as applying his skills to two-wheelers goes, Paddy began in the late Seventies with a 'godawful' two-stroke Suzuki 550, which gave way to a 750 Norton Commando, that, in turn, relinquished its position to his first serious build, a 1015 Rickman Kawasaki that weighed just 400 pounds and put out 130bhp ... about ten years ahead of Honda's FireBlade. As with his previous mounts, the Rickman had a dual role as both track and road bike, but while he was campaigning that bike, Paddy also found the time and wherewithal to create a custom Honda CBX that, at the time, impressed everyone, judges included, but which was impossible to categorise at any of the shows it appeared at (though it usually took the Best Engineering trophy for its trouble).

At heart he was an engineer and a racer, not a custom bike builder, so his attentions soon turned back to competition. Paddy knew what his ideal bike should be – narrow (so it would have fewer than three cylinders), of large capacity (1000ccs or more), and light.

A vee-twin would be good – they could hook up the back tyre on the track and maintain traction in adverse conditions thanks to the uneven power pulses. This left him with three choices: a Weslake (rare, and difficult to improve on), a Ducati (the front cylinder of which would prevent a short wheelbase necessary for twisty-turny hillclimbing), or ... a Harley – stupid idea, too slow, too heavy, but nevertheless superb in both dirt track racing and on the drag strip.

For no other reason than for the sheer hell of it Paddy chose to go the H-D route, and so began a series of different versions of Big Twin Evolution-powered machines that soon had fellow competitors and observers taking him seriously, very seriously. So much so, that his record-breaking performances prompted one race organisation to re-write their rule book just to keep Paddy and his bike out of the four-stroke twins class!

This latest incarnation was intended to make those same people sit up and take notice. As Paddy says, 'Who, in their right mind, would build a motorcycle out of titanium, magnesium and carbon fibre, using Grand Prix components that cost as much as a house, and then beat the life out of it on a hillclimb? Let's face it, a one-gallon tank and five miles per gallon isn't the product of a rational mind, is it? But you know what? I don't care!'

Turbo Katana

ENGINE:	SUZUKI GSX1100EFE PORTED AND FLOWED CYLINDER HEAD, TURBO/NITROUS CAMS, SLOTTED CAM SPROCKETS, OVERSIZE STAINLESS STEEL VALVES, 1327CC PISTONS, ORIENT EXPRESS UNDERCUT GEARBOX, KOSMAN OUTRIGGER BEARING SUPPORT, RAJAY TURBOCHARGER, ADJUSTABLE WASTEGATE, NITROUS WITH SCHNITZ PROGRAMMABLE NITROUS CONTROLLER, WATER/METHANOL INJECTION, S&S SHORTY CARB, MALLORY MAGNETO, MRE AIRSHIFTER
FRAME:	SUZUKI GSX 1100 KATANA, MODIFIED HEADSTOCK, BILLET FOOTREST MOUNTS
FRONT END:	SUZUKI GSX-R 400RL WHEEL, FORKS AND MODIFIED YOKES, TOKICO 6 POT CALIPERS, BILLET RISERS, SUZUKI GSX-R CLOCKS.
REAR END:	SPONDON EXTENDED SWINGARM WITH BUILT-IN AIRTANK, SUZUKI GSX-R 750WT 6" REAR WHEEL AND DISC, 190 SECTION TYRE, BREMBO MASTER-CYLINDER
BODYWORK:	MODIFIED SUZUKI GSX1100 KATANA

TURBO KATANA

THE REVITALIZED KATANA'S FIRST YEAR ON THE QUARTER MILE WAS SPENT EITHER GOING VERY QUICKLY, BUCKING LIKE A WILD HORSE OR BLOWING UP.

A few years ago Carl Lanscome ran a very trick Suzuki known as 'Krazy Kat' – a turbocharged, drag racing Katana. It was very competitive in its day (running 9.2 second quarter-miles), but then it became outclassed and dropped from the limelight. It was then rescued from obscurity by Sean at Big CC Racing and fettled to run in the Straightliners series with the Mad Count (a well-known eccentric Englishman) on board. To reach that level, Sean tore the bike down to its most basic components ... and then threw most of them away.

In fact, just about everything about the Kat – bar the swingarm, the seat and the gearbox – has been replaced. The headstock's been fully braced, as has the swingarm pivot area, and the whole plot fully lowered to aid stability on the strip. A GSX-R 400RL wheel, forks and yokes are fitted with a pair of EBC Pro-Lite discs and Tokico six pot calipers, along with Renntec bars in billet risers, and a fast-action Magura throttle. The swingarm is still the Spondon extended one with its built-in airtank from the 'Krazy Kat' days, but it now holds a six-inch wheel from a 750WT, and the suspension is either a pair of Koni shocks or lock-up struts, depending on how the bike's going to be used.

Turning to the engine – the head's been ported and flowed and fitted with Cam Motion turbo/nitrous cams and Orient Express slotted cam sprockets, heavy duty valve springs and extended tappet adjusters, Manley 1.5mm oversize stainless steel intake valves, Manley 1mm oversize stainless steel exhaust valves, a three-angle valve seat job, and Orient Express heavy-duty cylinder studs and APE nuts. Moving downwards, a Star Racing Gorilla block has been fitted with MTC 1327cc low compression turbo pistons and, for reliability, the liners have been piano-wired and all the cylinder and crankcase studs are both heavy duty and timeserted. The crank has been welded, pinned, balanced and fitted with Carillo con rods, and the oil pump's been uprated to a high flow/high pressure item as well. An Orient Express undercut gearbox with straight-cut primary gears and a billet lock-up clutch assembly transfers the power through a Kosman outrigger sprocket/bearing support, and a Mallory self-regulating magneto takes care of the sparks. And, finally, there's a Kosman alternator cover and remote starter assembly (because everything not needed has been removed) and an MRE air-shifter.

The Mr Turbo turbocharger kit has a modified Rajay unit, with a 17-30ft/lbs boost adjustable wastegate and a water/methanol injection kit with 10ft/lbs release valves to stop detonation at high revs. The fuel is fed through a Pingel Guzzler fuel tap via dual Facet fuel pumps and pro/flo regulators to an S&S Shorty carb with a billet bellmouth. Boosting the power still further is a throttle-activated NOS nitrous kit with Schnitz programmable nitrous controller.

The revitalized Katana's first year on the quarter mile was spent either going very quickly, bucking like a wild horse or blowing up.

WORLD BEATING RD

World Beating RD

MAKE & MODEL:	**YAMAHA RD400E**
ENGINE:	**YAMAHA RD400E HEADS WITH NEW COMBUSTION CHAMBERS, PORTED AND REWORKED 424CC BARRELS, REWORKED YAMAHA DT175 PISTONS, FBG LECTRON 38MM CARBS, EXHAUSTS BY SPEC PIPES, WELDED RD400 CRANK, CRANKCASES MACHINED AND PORTED, BILLET LOCK-UP CLUTCH, ONE-OFF CLUTCH CASE AND SIX-SPEED GEARBOX**
FRAME:	**KOSMAN PRO-STOCK REPLICA BY COLL RULE, ONE INCH GROUND CLEARANCE, ADJUSTABLE WHEELBASE TO SUIT TRACK AND CONDITIONS.**
FRONT END:	**KAWASAKI AR50 SHORTENED AND LIGHTENED FORKS, BILLET YOKES BY COLL RULE, LIGHTENED RG125 WHEEL, RG125 DISC, GRIMECA 2 POT CALIPER, PRO-STOCK ALLOY BARS, AR50 MASTER-CYLINDER, MRE AIRSHIFTER GAUGE**
REAR END:	**AMERICAN CCR 6.5" X 18" SPUN ALLOY WHEEL WITH BILLET CENTRE AND DISC, GRIMECA CALIPER**
BODYWORK:	**JADE RACING ONE-OFF CARBON-FIBRE FRONT MUDGUARD, TWO PINT (ONE QUART) ALLOY FUEL TANK, ONE-OFF CARBON-FIBRE TZR-BASED BODY AND FAIRING**
ELECTRICS:	**DYNA S IGNITION, ONE-OFF IGNITION BACK PLATE AND STARTER NUT, TWO-STAGE REV-LIMITER, IGNITION KILL LANYARD, TOP GEAR WARNING LIGHT**

POWER ISN'T THE BE-ALL AND END-ALL –
TOO MUCH WEIGHT AND YOU'RE GOING
NOWHERE FAST. SO THE CHASSIS IS
SUITABLY MINIMAL.

Many people would find it unbelievable that a motorcycle of a mere four hundred and twenty-four cee-cees could hold a world record. Or that a drag racing record could be held by someone other than an American, or by a bike not built in the States. Yet this little Yamaha is from the UK, as is Jerry Collier, its rider, and it is officially the world's quickest two-stroke motorcycle. It gained that title on August 30th 1998, at Avon Park in Warwickshire, when Jerry posted a 9.671 second quarter mile time at 134.33mph. And you must remember that this bike is normally aspirated and it doesn't use nitrous.

So what does it take to make such a small bike go so fast? The engine started as a standard RD400, was fitted with modified DT175 pistons in ported and reworked barrels, the heads are re-shaped RD items, and the bottom end is a welded RD400 crank in machined and ported cases. The motor breathes through a pair of Kawasaki six-petal reed blocks with carbon-fibre reeds, outboard of which sit a pair of 38mm Lectron flatslide carburettors. The very noisy expansion chambers are one-off up-and-overs by Spec Pipes, and are lagged to improve the power delivery and to protect the bodywork. The gearbox is a unique six-speed set-up, created by the use of RD, TZ and specially machined gears and utilises only three selectors rather than the standard four. The clutch is a billet lock-up affair that's adjustable in three ways to vary the way the bike launches off the line and how it changes gear. This little lot produces a proven 92bhp at the back wheel.

But power isn't the be-all and end-all – too much weight and you're going nowhere fast. So the chassis is suitably minimal. A Kosman Pro-Stock replica frame with shortened and lightened AR50 forks in billet yokes (with a lightened RG125 wheel and disc), a 6.5" spun alloy CCR wheel at the back, Grimeca calipers front and rear, carbon-fibre bodywork and only an airshifter gauge and top gear light for instrumentation all help to ensure the weight is kept as low as possible.

But attaining that record wasn't enough. Jade Racing (Jerry and his wife Sharron) are developing the bike still further, losing weight from the chassis and gaining power through the addition of an airbox and maybe nitrous oxide. This should see the bike crashing through the eight-second barrier.

Criag's KX500 (left)

ENGINE:	FULLY REBUILT, BOYESEN REEDS, TWIN CARBON CANS.
FRAME:	ONE-OFF SUBFRAME FOR PILLION FOOTRESTS.
FRONT END:	TZR250 WHEEL, HARRISON CALIPER.
REAR END:	TZR250 WHEEL AND DISC.
BODYWORK:	CUT-DOWN FRONT MUDGUARD, ACERBIS REAR MUDGUARD

Tom's CR500 (middle)

ENGINE:	504CC, WISECO PISTON AND RINGS, BOYESEN REED VALVE AND REEDS, SKIMMED AND POLISHED HEAD, TWO BASE GASKETS, SPLITFIRE PLUG, CARBON CLUTCH PLATES, PRO-CIRCUIT EXHAUST WITH TWIN CARBON CANS.
FRAME:	STANDARD
FRONT END:	REVALVED FORKS, 300MM PFM DISC, HARRISON CALIPER, 17" X 3.5" RIM.
REAR END:	17" X 4.5" RIM
BODYWORK:	YAMAHA TZR250 MUDGUARD, CUT DOWN REAR PANEL.

Mick's KX500 (right)

ENGINE:	WISECO PISTON, TWIN AIR FILTERS, BOYESEN REEDS.
FRAME:	STANDARD
FRONT END:	1990 SUZUKI RM FORKS, REWORKED YOKES, YAMAHA TZR250 WHEEL AND DISC, HONDA TWIN-POT CALIPER.
REAR END:	WP SHOCK, TZR250 WHEEL AND DISC
BODYWORK:	MXA SEAT, ACERBIS REAR GUARD

SUPERMOTARD THREESOME
THESE THREE SUPERMOTARDS ARE PERFECT EXAMPLES OF THEIR BREED...

These three supermotards are perfect examples of their breed, mixing and matching the best original equipment components with the choicest after-market accessories to create monster bikes that are the best balance of power, weight, cost and attitude available.

Tom's CR500 Honda (the white and purple one) is of 1990 vintage and is probably the one with the most modified engine. It's been bored to 504cc and fitted with a Wiseco piston and ring set, Boyesen reed valves and reeds, and two base gaskets separate the barrel from the cases. Combined with the Splitfire spark plug, these ensure the 500 single motor starts easily, usually at the second or third kick. Those two-stroke fumes are funnelled out through a chromed Pro-Circuit exhaust with twin carbon cans and all the water pipes and fittings are braided, alloy or stainless.

Like most supermotards the frame has been left as standard – it's competent enough when it leaves the factory – as has the front end, though the Showa forks

have been revalved and topped up with lighter weight oil for road use. The Honda disc has been replaced by a 300mm PFM disc that's gripped by a Harrison Billet Six caliper on a one-off hangar, and while Tom's kept the stock wheel hub, he has it laced to a much more suitable 17" x 3.5" rim via stainless spokes. The brake line's a Goodridge one, the speedo's from Sammy Miller, and the bars are Renthals.

At the back, a revalved stock shock is joined by a polished stock swingarm and linkage and an anodized stock rear brake with bronze sintered pads. The rear disc is stock too, and again the Honda hub has been laced to a 17" rim, this time 4.5" wide, but again with stainless spokes.

As it would be pointless changing the CR's plastics when the whole design idea behind a supermotard is 'motocrosser on the road', the only changes to the bodywork are a Yamaha TZR250 front mudguard and a cut-down rear panel.

Mick's KX500 is the blue and green one – it's a 1986 Kawasaki KX with a Wiseco piston, twin air filters, Boyesen reeds and a chromed exhaust pipe. Not

much, you may think, but if you've ever ridden a large capacity motocrosser on the road, then you'll know that that's more than enough. Ride a 500 on the road properly and race replicas will only pass you on the longest of straights.

Again the frame is stock, but the original forks have been replaced with 1990 Suzuki RM upside-downies, complete with three-spoke TZR250 wheel, with a matching 17 incher at the rear. The front disc is a 320mm item, gripped by a gold-anodised Honda twin-pot caliper, and the rear disc is TZR held by the standard KX caliper. The swingarm is KX and the shock's a WP unit. Excepting the MXA seat and Acerbis rear guard, the bodywork is standard, complete with Kawasaki 'green meanie' colour scheme.

That leaves Criag's KX — the all-green one. His 1987 500C has been fully rebuilt with a new piston and ring set, and fitted with fully polished Boyesen reeds. The carb's been chromed to match the extremely shiny trick exhaust system with its twin carbon cans, and all the water and fuel lines are from Goodridge.

Unusually though, the frame on this KX has been altered — the stock subframe has been chopped off and in its place a subtly different one added. 'Crossers aren't famed for their pillion comforts, but Criag wanted the option of taking someone along for the ride. Again, TZR250 wheels and discs are used, with a Harrison Billet Six caliper up front and the KX unit at the back.

Revenge DTR

ENGINE:	RD350 YPVS WITH K&N FILTER AND REJETTED MIKUNI CARBS, STANDARD RD EXHAUSTS ALTERED TO FIT, RE-SLEEVED CANS, COMPETITION REEDS
FRAME:	1991 DTR WITH ONE-OFF CRADLE, NEW ENGINE MOUNTS AND BRACING
FRONT END:	REVALVED DTR FORKS, HEAVY FORK OIL, EXTENDED PRELOAD SPACERS, TDR250 HUB, STAINLESS SPOKES, AKRONT RIM, FZR1000 DISC AND 4 POT CALIPER, RENTHAL MOTOCROSS BARS
REAR END:	CHROMED DTR SWINGARM, RM250 DAMPER WITH DTR SPRING WITH LARGE ALLOY SPACER (FULLY ADJUSTABLE), DTR HUB WITH STAINLESS SPOKES AND AKRONT RIM, STANDARD DTR BRAKE
BODYWORK:	STANDARD DTR, DTR FUEL TANK WITH RECESSED ALLOY FILLER CAP

REVENGE DTR

SHOEHORNING A YAMAHA 350YPVS ENGINE INTO A DTR FRAME FROM THE SAME MARQUE IS PROBABLY THE EPITOME OF THIS 'BEAUTY AND THE BEAST' TYPE STYLING.

The idea behind the Supermotard streetfighter movement is to create something that looks as graceful and delicate as a ballerina, yet packs a punch like a world heavyweight boxing champion. Shoehorning a Yamaha 350YPVS engine into a DTR frame from the same marque is probably the epitome of this 'beauty and the beast' type styling.

The project began when Tom Oliver's girlfriend walked out after he'd made the ultimate gesture and bought her a bike so she could learn to ride. Undeterred, he took out his hacksaw and cut up her little DTR, then began scouting round for something interesting to power it. Big Four Engineering heard of his venture and offered him a tricked-up YPVS unit to slide in the hole he had made and everyone agreed that at the very least, this should make things highly entertaining. One would imagine that fitting what is essentially a two-stroke racing engine between the skinny rails of a trail bike frame would be quite a task. Not so. Tom simply cut away the frame below the headstock, forward of the footrests, and offered the meaty

lump up on a trolley jack before welding the necessary mounting plates around it. Indeed, the hardest part was maintaining the classic DTR look of the overall machine.

Virtually all of the running gear is from the original DTR – it has just been up-rated and strengthened to cope with the oodles of extra power that the YPVS motor is going to transmit through to the tarmac. But despite this sensible approach to controlling the power of the machine during the build-up, Tom felt the need to test his steed when it sported nothing more than a powerful engine in a skinny frame with one brake and a 52 toothed rear sprocket. It doesn't require a rocket scientist to imagine the results – suffice to say that getting the front wheel to point skyward was a lot easier than getting both wheels to stay on the road.

The finished article is a real treat. It looks like a very clean and tidy DTR shod with road-going rubber, with only the extra low level pipe giving the game away. But when you get close, or you're sitting next to it at the lights, you're in for a very big surprise indeed.

Super M Yamada

ENGINE	1991 YAMAHA XT600E, REBUILT, STOCK AIRBOX, ONE-OFF STAINLESS STEEL EXHAUST WITH ONE-OFF CARBON SILENCERS
FRAME	ERW TUBULAR STEEL, TRIANGULATED FORM, HONDA HEAD STOCK AND SWINGARM PIVOT POINTS
FRONT END	HONDA CBR600FM WHEEL, PIRELLI DRAGON 120 X 17 CORSA, HONDA CR500 USD FORKS, BILLET ALLY YOKES, HONDA VFR750 300MM DISC, BILLET CALIPER CARRIER, YAMAHA EXUP CALIPER/MASTER CYLINDER, XT CLOCKS, RENTHAL BARS
REAR END	HONDA CBR600FM WHEEL, PIRELLI DRAGON 160 X17 CORSA, HONDA CR500 SWINGARM, CBR600 DISC, CR500 CALIPER/MASTER CYLINDER, ONE-OFF ADJUSTABLE SUSPENSION LINKAGE WITH UPRATED SHOCK
BODYWORK	DUCATI 900SS FRONT MUDGUARD, MODIFIED CBR600 CARBON REAR HUGGER, BAFFLED UNDERSEAT FUEL TANK WITH ZZR600 FILLER CAP, CR500 TANK COVER AND SIDEPANELS, MODIFIED CR500 SEAT
ENGINEERING	EVERYTHING EXCEPT PAINT AND PIPES BY OWNER

SUPER M YAMADA

THERE ARE THOSE WHO THROW THE RULEBOOK OUT OF THE WINDOW AND DiVE HEADLONG iNTO THE MURKY WATERS OF OBSESSiON, SACRiFiCiNG EVERYTHiNG iN THE PURSUiT OF EXCELLENCE.

There are, in life, varying degrees of dedication. Some of us like to merely dip our toes into the waters of our chosen passions, indulging our flights of fancy in a moderate and restrained fashion. Then there are those who throw the rulebook (and, in some cases, most of a donor motorcycle) out of the window and dive headlong into the murky waters of obsession, sacrificing everything in the pursuit of excellence.

Chris Whitworth falls into the latter category and his beautiful Super M stands as testament to this. Almost four years in the making, Chris began the project back in 1994, when he picked up a Honda CR500 rolling chassis for a very reasonable price at his local breaker's yard. After ditching virtually everything and constructing a one-off jig to replicate his own version of Honda's cradle from ERW, Chris began the lengthy and detailed task of creating the bike that existed, at the time, only in his head.

One might find it strange to discover that Chris reckoned he was a bit of an engineering dunce, but he overcame his perceived handicap by enrolling on a one-year NVQ course, which gave him the skills to braze and machine parts that a skilled engineer of some years standing would probably baulk at. Armed with his new-found knowledge, he cut and widened the swingarm to take the larger CBR600 rear wheel complete with stiffened and fully adjustable rear shock, whilst the front sports a set of hand-made billet yokes, CR500 USD forks and the other wheel from the CBR.

Fitting the totally rebuilt 1991 XT600 engine into a very restricted frame space required some lateral thinking to redesign virtually the whole layout of the bike. XT engines have always worked best with the standard airbox in place, but this left no room for the fuel tank, which was a fairly major problem. Solution? Fit a one-off unit over the tail, with the rear light loom running through an integral conduit. The tank's been baffled to prevent sloshing and because the carbs are no longer gravity fed it's been fitted with a solid state fuel pump, too. The now-redundant space above the engine houses the air-box and all the usual ancillary components needed to make the whole thing go.

There are a million and one little touches that make this machine stand out – the one-off U-shaped oil tank that holds four litres of lubricant for the dry sump motor, the side-panels that have been scooped to force air across the top of the engine, the unique stainless pipe and carbon can that looks absolutely stunning. But perhaps the most attractive and also restrained feature is the fairing. Chris made a mock-up on the bike, shaping, cutting, refining, and then when he was totally happy, he created a mould from body-filler and cast his own fibre-glass unit.

It's this kind of dedication that has won him awards for his beautiful machine, but the awards are just a nice finishing touch – the real reward is the bike itself.

Yamaha RD350LC

ENGINE: YAMAHA RD350LC YPVS F2, PRO-CUT GEARBOX, HEAVY-DUTY CLUTCH, PRO-PORTING ONE-OFF EXHAUSTS AND CARBON CANS, MODIFIED CARBURETTORS WITH K&N FILTERS, YAMAHA TDM850 RADIATOR, YAMAHA TZR250 THERMOSTAT

FRAME: ONE-OFF FRAME FABRICATED IN CDS BY KESMARK MOTORCYCLES, BILLET ALUMINIUM REAR-SETS WITH YAMAHA RD350 YPVS FOOTRESTS

FRONT END: SUZUKI RGV250N USD FORKS, RE-VALVED AND RE-SPRUNG. RGV250N YOKES, HONDA NC30 WHEEL, HONDA CBR900 BRAKE DISCS, HONDA RVF400 NC35 BRAKE MASTER

REAR END: HONDA VFR750FN SINGLE-SIDED SWINGING-ARM, SUSPENSION LINKAGES, WHEEL AND CALIPER, FABRICATED ONE-OFF RIDE-HEIGHT ADJUSTER AND BILLET ALUMINIUM TORQUE ARM. SHOWA NC30 SUSPENSION UNIT

BODYWORK: YAMAHA FZR250 FUEL TANK WITH PINGEL HI-FLOW TWIN OUTLET TAP, APRILIA RS250 SEAT UNIT, RS250 FAIRING, SUZUKI RGV250N FRONT MUDGUARD, CARBON FIBRE REAR HUGGER

YAMAHA RD350LC

THE SEAT UNIT AND FAIRING CONTAIN THE ORIGINAL RS LIGHTS BUT THE INDICATOR LIGHTS HAVE BEEN REPLACED WITH ITEMS FROM A CAR.

The bare bones that make up the essentials of a streetfighter need consist of no more than a factory standard bike with a reputation. But it goes without saying that the more time and money that is spent on that reputable standard machine then the more of a streetfighter it becomes.

Nige Kimber started his project with a bike that many consider to be the ultimate hooligan tool of the early Eighties – the Yamaha 350LC. He then took a well-chosen selection of the very best parts donated by late model versions of many of the best Japanese and Italian small capacity race replicas, and, using the perfect and precise handling of a British-made chassis, created the ultimate two-stroke 'fighter.

The frame itself is a one-off duplex steel trellis, chosen for its light weight and easy engine access, and created by Kesmark Motorcycles. The front end is a reworked Suzuki RGV250N, the forks have been re-valved and re-sprung to suit the reduced weight and altered balance, and the front brake calipers have been modified to fit the FireBlade discs that mount to the Honda NC30 (VFR400) front wheel. They are operated by a master cylinder from the factory RC45 race kit. The rear end is a VFR750N single-sided swinging-arm, with suspension linkages, wheel and caliper all taken from Honda's supreme sports-tourer. The brake disc and hub assembly wheel have been skimmed and lightened to fit in with the whole ethic of

the bike (ie smaller/lighter/faster), and the rear end follows that formula with a Showa-manufactured, NC30-sourced rear shock, with a VFR brake operated by an NSR250 rear master cylinder.

The bodywork is almost entirely a Latin affair, with only the FZR250 petrol tank breaking up the Aprilia RS250 plastics. The seat unit and fairing contain the original RS lights but the indicator lights have been replaced with items from a four-wheeler – a Ford Ka, to be precise.

The engine started life in a Yamaha RD350LC, from a YPVS model, so it came complete with the power-enhancing Powervalves. It was fettled with the aid of ported cylinders, skimmed and re-profiled cylinder heads, and ported waterways to help the cooling. The crankshaft was balanced and a pair of Pro-Porting expansion chambers and silencer cans were fitted, along with a heavy duty clutch and GSX-R1100 output bearing and offset gearbox sprocket.

The resulting ensemble fits together well enough to resemble a factory-produced homologation special, particularly with the subtle and understated paintwork – except the only motorcycle factory to produce a road-going two-stroke twin homologation special with lights was Bimota and their short-lived V-Due, and the built quality of this LC exceeds even that of the Rimini-produced Bimotas.

Yamaha RD350	
ENGINE:	YAMAHA RD350 YPVS, S&B FILTERS, SWARBRICK EXPANSION CHAMBERS WITH CARBON FIBRE END CANS, HI-TECH RACING REEDS
FRAME:	MODIFIED YAMAHA RD350LC
FRONT END:	YAMAHA TZR250 FRONT END, EARL'S STAINLESS STEEL HOSES, MODIFIED YAMAHA RD350LC YOKES, RENTHAL 'BARS, MINI SPEEDO AND REV COUNTER, STOCK HEADLAMP, YAMAHA RD350 YPVS SWITCHGEAR
REAR END:	ONE-OFF JMC SWINGARM, EMC RACE SHOCK, YAMAHA TZR250 WHEEL AND X, EARL'S STAINLESS STEEL HOSE, ONE-OFF STAINLESS TORQUE ARM, BMX STUNT 'PEGS AS REAR FOOTRESTS
BODYWORK:	YAMAHA TZR250 FRONT MUDGUARD, YAMAHA RD350LC TANK, SEAT AND TAILPIECE, STAINLESS ELECTRICS BOX BY TIM AT RUSKIN FABRICATION

YAMAHA RD350

LOVE THEM OR LOATHE THEM, YOU CAN'T IGNORE THEM, ESPECIALLY IF THEY'RE BRIGHT YELLOW AND HEADING YOUR WAY WAILING LIKE A BANSHEE, THE FRONT WHEEL POINTING SKYWARDS AND A SMOKE HAZE TRAILING BEHIND.

Between 1980 and 1983 Yamaha sold over 6500 examples of the RD350LC. Most were raced, either on the street or the track – or both – a high percentage were crashed and are now found lurking in the back of breakers' yards or in garden sheds across the land.

This one is an LC2, the first of the new class of 1983, when it was a recipe for carnage. An old frame and a new engine meant more tankslappers and more bikes turning up at the breakers. LC or YPVS – love them or loathe them, you can't ignore them, especially if they're bright yellow and heading your way wailing like a banshee, the front wheel pointing skywards, and a smoke haze trailing behind. Back in '83 this would have been the bike to drool over, the one to have the girls gathering in their droves.

Matthew Mullinder, the owner of this particular YPVS, was only ten years old back then, but he was still heavily influenced enough to hang onto the Eighties' dream and build this bike. Finally, once he'd reached both the right age and the right financial standing, he came across a rather standard, rather bland YPVS. Initially he had visions of grandeur – big-bore, trick suspension, garish paint – but finances dictated otherwise (although working part-time in his father's motorcycle

shop did have its advantages). So, in order to preserve the contents of his wallet and the crankcases, he left the famous production race-winning internals alone, although a pair of Swarbricks' gorgeous hand-built expansion chambers with carbon fibre end cans were fitted to release any power trapped by the standard exhausts. And that was to be it – save for a couple of S&B filters and a set of Hi-Tech racing reeds, the rest remains as it left the factory.

A complete TZR250 front end was sourced and fitted along with Earl's hoses and Renthal handlebars, transforming the ex-clip-on equipped, head-down tankslapper into the wheelie monster it is today. With the front end thus tamed, the rear was next on his list. So he fitted an ex-CR500 EMC shock which was linked to a one-off JMC swingarm. The standard 110 rear rubber was replaced by a larger 130 rear from a TZR250 (again) and the rear footrests were taken off and replaced with pegs from his younger brother's BMX and bolted onto the Yam.

The bodywork and electrics are as Yamaha intended, barring the TZR front mudguard, but they've been trimmed, lightened and cleaned up to look far neater than when they first rolled off the production line more than seventeen long years ago.

Gamma RG500

ENGINE: 1986 SUZUKI RG500, 570 BIG BORE, STAN STEPHENS STAGE III HEADS & BARRELS, MODIFIED AIRBOX, MODIFIED INLET TRACTS, CARBS BORED TO 31.5MM, RICK LANCE FILTER KIT, 240 MAINS, CHROMED & POLISHED NIKON FULL-RACE EXPANSION PIPES, ONE-OFF WATER INJECTION SYSTEM, 130BHP AT THE BACK WHEEL

FRAME: 1986 SUZUKI RG500, MODIFIED REAR SUBFRAME, TAROZZI REARSETS

FRONT END: SUZUKI RGV250M WHEEL, FORKS, YOKES, BRAKES & HANDLE-BARS, KAWASAKI ZX6-R MASTER-CYLINDERS, BRAIDED BRAKELINES, MODIFIED RG500 SWITCHGEAR, SPA THREE STAGE PROGRAMMABLE SHIFT LIGHT, RG500 CLOCKS, ONE-OFF INSTRUMENT SURROUND BY OWNER, BLUE ANODISED INDICATORS

REAR END: SUZUKI RG500 SWINGARM, ÖHLINS TYPE 4 SHOCK, SUZUKI RGV250M WHEEL, RG500 BRAKE, BRAIDED BRAKELINE, B&C ONE-OFF SPROCKETS, BLUE ANODISED INDICATORS

BODYWORK: SUZUKI RGV250M FRONT MUDGUARD & SIDEPANELS & FAIRING, SUZUKI RG500 PETROL TANK, DUCATI 916 REPLICA SEAT UNIT

ENGINEERING: ALL WORK BY OWNER

GAMMA RG500

FROM THE MOMENT IT HIT THE STREETS, ANYBODY WHO HAD EVER HARBOURED A DESIRE TO BE LIKE FAST FREDDY SPENCER BOUGHT ONE AND PROCEEDED TO ANNOY THE HELL OUT OF THEIR NEIGHBOURS AT THREE IN THE MORNING UNTIL THEY WRAPPED THEMSELVES AND IT ROUND A TREE.

It's strange, but some bikes you just know are going to be classics the minute they roll off the production line. The GSX-R 750, for instance, or Kwaka's GPz 1100 – and this little beauty, Suzuki's gorgeous, perfectly formed RGV500 Gamma race rep.

From the moment it hit the streets, anybody who had ever harboured a desire to be like Fast Freddy Spencer bought one and proceeded to annoy their neighbours at three in the morning until they wrapped themselves and it around a tree. Consequently fine examples of this outrageously lovely machine are becoming few and far between and highly sought after.

Mark's beautiful bike underwent the same sort of fate. Although spared from a front end engagement with an immovable object, it had been used and abused and then put in a damp garage and left to rot for the next six years. He picked the bike up for £175, which tells its own story as to the bike's condition. Mark was going to simply get it going and thrash it into the ground as a fun bike, but something as beautiful and elegant as a Gamma has to be treated with the respect it deserves, so

there began a lengthy and expensive restoration and improvement process.

The front end was swapped in its entirety for an RGV250 set-up (which conveniently bolts straight on) and the original but extremely tatty, and in some cases non-existent, bodywork was also swapped for its little sister's clothes. The rear has been treated to a one-off Öhlins overhaul to radically improve the handling.

The engine was essentially blueprinted and then given to Stan Stevens for a stage three tune to the cylinder head, barrels and rotary valves. This is quite a serious tune for a road-going two-stroke, but amazingly, another 18BHP has been found by using a water injection system. The four number 70 Mikuni jets squirt water into the exhaust chamber (at full throttle) in precisely metered amounts and combined with that radical tune, produces a staggering 130BHP at the rear wheel.

This is probably one of the most satisfying projects around, not just because it's a beautiful bike that has been rescued and restored, but because it now outclasses the original and will take on any of the modern big boys despite its now elderly status. Long live the spirit of Fast Freddy.

THE ULTiMATE

V-Max in Gold

ENGINE:	1997 YAMAHA V-MAX, 1300CC, JE PISTONS, GASFLOWED HEADS, REPROFILED CAMS, CARILLO RODS, BARNETT CLUTCH, FACET FUEL PUMP, GARRETT T2.5 TURBO, FULL-WIDTH INTERCOOLER, OWNER-MADE ALUMINIUM PLENUM CHAMBER, NITROUS EXPRESS 60BHP KIT, STANDARD CARBS WITH STAGE 7 DYNOJET
FRAME:	STOCK 1997 YAMAHA V-MAX FRONT CRADLE, ONE-OFF REAR SECTION. ENGINE MOUNTS MODIFIED TO ALLOW FOR 2.5MM OFFSET, HARRIS ADJUSTABLE REARSETS
FRONT END:	OWNER-MODIFIED ZX-7R WHEEL, YAMAHA THUNDERACE SPEEDO DRIVE, EBC PRO-LITE DISCS, BREMBO MASTER CYLINDERS AND CALIPERS, WHITE POWER FORKS, RENTHAL DRAG BARS ON ONE-OFF RISERS
REAR END:	ONE-OFF SUBFRAME, ADJUSTABLE SHOWA SHOCK, THREE INCH OVER SWINGARM WITH BUILT-IN AIRTANK, ONBOARD COMPRESSOR, MODIFIED REAR DRIVE UNIT WITH OVERSIZE SPINDLE, OWNER-MODIFIED 8" WIDE ZX-7R WHEEL, EBC DISC, BREMBO CALIPER, HARRIS MASTER CYLINDER
BODYWORK:	APRILIA FRONT GUARD, ONE-OFF SIDEPODS (POLISHED ALUMINIUM TRUMPETS WITH FIBREGLASS BODY), ONE-OFF FIBRE GLASS NOSE FAIRING, ONE-OFF ONE-PIECE 22LTR TANK/SEAT UNIT
ELECTRICS:	ONE-OFF LOOM BY OWNER
PAINT:	NISSAN COPPER ORANGE BY OWNER
POLISHING:	OWNER/WESSEX POLISHING
THANKS TO:	'ROB COLGATE OF COLGATE ENGINEERING FOR ALL THE WELDING (AND SOMETIMES GOOD ADVICE)'

V-MAX iN GOLD

THE NiTROUS BUTTON HAS BEEN BUiLT iNTO ONE OF THE STOCK SWiTCHGEAR HOUSiNGS ... AND iT CARRiES A GOVERNMENT HEALTH WARNiNG.

ndy Griffith is a bit of a horsepower freak, so he decided that for his new V-Max a mixture of drag and streetfighter styles might work well. This bike, then, needed to be longer than standard, lower than standard, and have some serious power.

The turbo is a very special Garrett T2.5 which has modified vanes to suit the engine's capacity and power requirements, and Andy built his own blow-through system and connected from the exhaust outlets to the plenum chamber via an inter-cooler — the only way to go to get as many horses as possible from your turbocharged engine.

Due to the position of the turbo unit, the stock fuel tank was removed, to be replaced by a one-piece tank/seat unit which hinges upwards to allow access to the engine, and have quick-release fixings. The monster swingarm is now three inches over stock, as is the driveshaft, which has been modified to allow it to align with the gearbox shaft as well as the rear wheel. Andy wanted a 200 section rear tyre. The only trouble is that no-one makes a rear wheel for the V-Max that'll take a 200 section tyre.

'No problem,' said Andy, 'I'll just make one'... Taking two ZX-7R rear wheels, he removed four inches of rim section from one and welded it to the other to produce one eight-inch wide wheel. Then he bored out the middle and fitted a machined-down shaft-drive hub. However, a quick alignment check revealed a

major problem — with the tyre being so wide, the shaft still didn't want to mate with the engine's final drive. There was only one thing to do, move the engine. A few spacers later, the engine was repositioned three millimetres to the left, and alignment was achieved.

The front end is basically a White Power set-up, sporting Brembo stoppers and EBC Prolite discs. The ZX-7R front wheel had to receive a few machining mods, though, to allow the fitting of a ThunderAce speedo drive and, as per normal, everything's polished all over.

With the engine and rolling chassis sorted, Andy began the bodywork that would reflect the original V-Max shapes. He began with the side-pods. The idea here was to have a drag-style air intake pod, but which would hold driving lamps instead, in this case a pair of PIAA Iridium units which are switched to operate as low beam. The mini nose-cone also houses a pair of driving lamps but this time PIAA Diachronic ones, wired for main beam.

The bellypan hides the front-mounted battery, and the rear hugger follows the contours of the tyre and, by mounting underneath the swingarm, also hides the air compressor. The speedometer has been modified to include a wrap-round gearshift indicator, and the air-shift button and pressure gauge are also mounted at eye level. The nitrous button has been built into one of the stock switchgear housings... and it carries a government health warning.

Sculpture Ducati

MAKE & MODEL:	DUCATI 600SS
ENGINE:	DUCATI 600SS
FRAME:	ONE-OFF STEEL TRELLIS
FRONT END:	DUCATI FORKS, DUCATI WHEEL AND SINGLE DISC, BREMBO CALIPER
REAR END:	MODIFIED DUCATI SWINGARM, DUCATI WHEEL, BREMBO CALIPER
BODYWORK:	HAND-BEATEN ALUMINIUM SHEET BY OWNER
ELECTRICS:	OFFSIDE FAIRING HOLDS FUSE BOX, FUEL PUMP AND STARTER RELAY, NEARSIDE FAIRING HOLDS THE REST.
POLISHING/PLATING:	LOTS. EVERYWHERE. ALL BY OWNER.
ENGINEERING:	ALTHOUGH GENERALLY A STANDARD BIKE MECHANICALLY, LOTS OF HIDDEN WORK, ALL BY OWNER.
THANKS TO:	EVERYONE CONCERNED

SCULPTURE DUCATI

HE STARTED OFF WITH A STANDARD, COMPLETE DUCATI 600SS, TOOK THE ENGINE, ELECTRICS, FORKS, SWINGARM WHEELS AND BRAKES AND PROMPTLY SCRAPPED THE REST.

There is no doubt that the Italians have the best auto-designers in the world. From Ferraris and Lamborghinis to the Ducati 916 and Supermono and the MV Agusta F4, each is a masterpiece of design. Yet all of them pale in comparison alongside Codutti Ferruccio's Ducati 600.

Codutti is a master of his trade — his trade being hand-forming aluminium sheet, and this bike is not only a platform for those panel beating skills, but also for his talents as a machinist, an auto-electrician and a stylist.

He started off with a standard, complete Ducati 600SS, took the engine, electrics, forks, swingarm wheels and brakes and promptly scrapped the rest. The frame is a one-off steel trellis affair in a similar vein to the original item, but the resemblance ends there.

The hand-beaten body panels include the front fairing/fly screen with ram-air scoops to the airbox, the side fairings (which also hold all of the electrics) with their built-in mirrors, the seat unit, the panel that covers the clock surround, the chainguard, the rear hugger and the front mudguard. The seat unit is actually the fuel tank, and the billet cap at the rear of the seat was a useful aid in enabling the seat unit to be shaped to suit.

Parts machined from solid aluminium billet include the clock surround, the sprocket cover, the engine mountings, the exhaust clamps, the mount for the rear reservoir hanger, the cam covers with the clamp for holding the hydraulic clutch pipe, the boss for holding the oil pressure wire away from that stunning billet oil cooler, the vacuum banjos, the steering lock-stops that are mounted off the frame onto stock but modified yokes, and the side stand is an exact replica of the stock item, but made of billet ally (and it folds away rather neatly into the bellypan, too).

Yet after all of this, there are still some standard parts on the 600, although most of them have, admittedly, felt the kiss of the grinder or the pillar drill. The Ducati swingarm, for example, has been cut and shut by 30mm, while the original rear shock has had the reservoir removed, turned around and refitted so that it follows the lines of the bike. The Ducati rear caliper hanger has been drilled and the billet footrests sit on tube hangers with eccentric cams to adjust the rear brake position. The stainless drive sprocket is drilled and slotted and sits on the stock carrier, which also happens to be machined and slotted. The exhaust system is a one-off in steel. Every bolt is waisted as far as possible and the original gear linkage has been smoothed and lightened. And to complete the bike Codutti took some of Mrs Ferruccio's lingerie to obtain the grey metalflake material to cover the seat! In all, this two-wheeled piece of automotive art took Codutti a mere 730 hours from start to finish.

Rotary Norton

ENGINE:	1986 NORTON ROTARY, TWIN 36MM AMAL CONCENTRIC SMOOTHBORE CARBS, PIPERCROSS AIRFILTERS, PIERCE CORE FILTER, NORTON FIVE SPEED GEARBOX, NORTON MULTI-PLATE DIAPHAGRAM CLUTCH, BOYER BRANSDEN IGNITION, NORTON RACE TEAM-DEVELOPED EXHAUST AND COOLING SYSTEM BY PETE GIBSON
POWER OUTPUT:	135BHP AT REAR WHEEL (ACCORDING TO THE NORTON RACE TEAM)
FRAME:	1992 YAMAHA FZR 1000 EXUP, EXUP FOOTRESTS AND HANGERS, MODIFIED SUBFRAME
FRONT END:	HONDA CBR900RR FIREBLADE WHEEL, BRAKES AND FORKS, ONE-OFF YOKES, RENNTEC BARS, YAMAHA MASTER-CYLINDERS, SUZUKI BANDIT SWITCHGEAR, NORTON F1 SPEEDO, NORTON INTERPOL TEMP GAUGES, ONE-OFF INSTRUMENT SURROUND
REAR END:	YAMAHA FZR 1000 EXUP SWINGARM WITH A ONE-OFF BRACE, EXUP SHOCK WITH REMOTE CYLINDER, HONDA CBR900RR FIREBLADE WHEEL AND BRAKE
BODYWORK:	HONDA CBR900RR CARBON FRONT MUDGUARD, MODIFIED

ROTARY NORTON

145MPH CRUISING WAS EASY, AND HE SOON FOUND THAT NOT ONLY DID IT BELCH MASSIVE BLUE FLAMES OUT OF THE EXHAUST ON THE OVER-RUN, BUT IT ALSO BLEW NATTY LITTLE SMOKE RINGS OUT OF IT WHILE IT WAS WARMING UP TOO.

This story starts back in 1997, when Geoff Madden had shoe-horned a Norton rotary engine into a Yamaha EXUP frame and equipped it with a FireBlade front and EXUP rear ends. He took the newly-finished and barely-running special to the Classic & Motorcycle Mechanics show at Stafford in October to put it on the Norton Owners' Club Stand to show his technological marvel to the masses. The 'Speed Trochoid,' as Geoff had dubbed it, was a stunning success, greatly impressing everyone who saw it.

The only trouble was that, as mentioned, the rotary was just barely running, and as the Wankel engine is a rare entity, there are very few people around with any experience of them. In fact, there was really only one man available for the job of fine tuning the motor – Kev Pierce of Pierce Tuning on Anglesey.

Kev took one look at the motor and declared the carbs and the rotor seals (responsible for the rotary engine's compression) entirely useless. So a brand new set of carbs was procured and the engine sideplates (which the rotors seal against) were moly-coated – a process that involves machining a one centimetre groove in the aluminium sideplates and filling it with molten molybdenum, which is then ground flush with the face. This is a great improvement over stock because, when the rotors overheat or are starved of oil, they try to weld them-

selves to the sideplates and cause the motor to seize. However, the molybdenum coating acts as a solid lubricant, preventing seizures from happening, with the added bonus of making everything run cooler as well.

With the motor rebuilt and run in, Kev set it up for high speed running. Geoff took it away and was just amazed by it – 145mph cruising was easy, and he soon found that not only did it belch massive blue flames out of the exhaust on the over-run, but it also blew natty little smoke rings out of it while it was warming up too. This is down to that very clever exhaust system. On any conventional Norton rotary, the way the engine is cooled limits the available power because the rotors are internally cooled by an airstream that's sucked through the centre of the engine on its way to the carbs – so the air that eventually gets to the carbs is warm and oily. Using a trick devised by the Norton race team, Geoff had a set of replica works Norton exhausts made for his road bike. This system uses the low pressure pulses in the exhaust to suck cool, clean air through the centre of the rotors, thus letting the carbs breathe their own supply of fresh air, thereby boosting the power from about 85bhp to 130+bhp and creating the now well-known firework display when the throttle's shut off.

Jet Trike

WHEN THE STARTER IS ENGAGED, THE JET ENGINE SPINS AT 10,500RPM UNTIL IT FIRES. IT THEN JUMPS TO A TICKOVER OF 25,000RPM AND WILL SPIN TO A MAXIMUM OF 38,000RPM.

THE LAST WORD IN EXTREME

Paul Bailey, having cut his teeth building trikes that were brilliant in their technical complexity, decided that he wanted to build the world's first and only road legal jet-engined trike.

To build this trike, Paul bought a complete (and roadworthy) SDI Rover in order to acquire its tuned 230bhp V8 engine, while the 4:1:1 rear axle came from a Daimler Sovereign in a similar road-going condition. The next job on the agenda was to take the motor and the back axle down to Chris Ireland, probably the UK's most respected trike builder. Chris specialises in seven-litre Buick-engined trikes, nitrous oxide-injected Mercedes V8 trikes, supercharged 350bhp V8 Rover trikes, fuel-injected V12 Jaguar trikes, so he was just the man for the job.

Chris fabricated the frame rails, the leading-link forks and the petrol tank, and narrowed the rear axle by 14inches. However, soon after he'd received the chassis back, Paul decided to alter it fairly dramatically by adding a full seven and a half inches to the front. He also made new underslung engine-to-chassis mounts, and relocated the rear suspension mounts to alter the ride height because, once the additional weight of the Rolls-Royce Paluste MK10 jet engine and fuel tanks had been entered into the equation, the back end was sitting rather low.

It was at about this point that he approached jet guru Martin Hill for help with the project. Martin runs the jet-powered drag car 'Fireforce' and is probably the most experienced, knowledgeable and capable jet-mechanic, engineer and designer outside of the aircraft industry.

Martin turned out to be just the catalyst Paul needed to get 'Colossus' finished. During his frequent visits to his workshop, he fabricated all the aluminium items in air-craft-quality alloy, including the pannier fuel tanks which hold the jet fuel, the air intakes, the small catch-tank and the dashboard. Not only that, but he also made up the stainless exhaust system for the V8 motor, and re-mounted and connected up the jet engine.

When the starter is engaged, the jet engine spins at 10,500rpm until it fires. It then jumps to a tickover of 25,000rpm and will spin to a maximum of 38,000rpm. And, when the afterburner is lit, the temperature in the jet pipe reaches 1000 degrees almost instantly. On full boost, fuel is pumped into the jet at 1500psi — that's five gallons per minute!

With the jet running and the boost pump engaged, the trike lays down huge clouds of unburnt fuel in a matter of seconds and then, with a thud so loud it shakes the air around it, ignites the mixture into a bellowing, roaring orange flame.

Colossus requires no outside assistance whatsoever to fire up either the road engine or the jet, and it's used regularly on the road and driven to most events at which Paul gives demonstration fire displays. What's more, Colossus is due to get even more extreme — Paul's already planning to fit a supercharger and a nitrous kit to the V8 road motor.